# Why We Teach

## Learning, Laughter, Love, and the Power to Transform Lives

# LINDA ALSTON

**■SCHOLASTIC**

NEW YORK • TORONTO • LONDON • AUCKLAND • SYDNEY
MEXICO CITY • NEW DELHI • HONG KONG • BUENOS AIRES

*To the strong spirit warriors from my womb,*

*my sons,*

*Courtney, Macio, and Joshua*

*Credits*

Photo, cover, Kevin Moloney.

Photo, page 42, courtesy of Hornbil Images/Alamy.

Photo, page 117, courtesy of Scripps Howard News Service.

Photo, page 131, courtesy of Cyrus McCrimmon/The Denver Post

Acquisition editor, Lois Bridges

Development editor, Danny Miller

Production editor, Sarah Longhi

Cover design by Maria Lilja

Interior design by Melinda Belter

ISBN-13 978-0-545-04705-0

ISBN-10 0-545-04705-6

1 2 3 4 5 6 7 8 9 10      23      15 14 13 12 11 10 09 08

# Acknowledgments

ॐ

I offer my profound gratitude to the following people:

My editor and sage, Lois Bridges, for this process and fruition because you believed in me from our first phone conversation. You're simply the best, and I give you my heart. People can only win around you; The DM'ster, Danny Miller for your exactitude, cultural competence, and courage to stand your ground; Sarah Longhi, for your kindness and indulgence in my playful banter; Terry Cooper, for your crystal clear vision, leadership, and for the "cool" in you. To all the people at Scholastic who were doulas in the birthing of this book and my dream of being an author. To my angel, the glamorous and beautiful Sue Lubeck for your nurturing, your concern, and for holding me high; Steph Harvey for listening to Sue and speaking your word for me in faith. For your enthusiasm about me that was so passionate it caused Lois to drive around lost in the parking lot when she picked you up at the airport.

To my ancestor, Dr. Mary McLeod Bethune, upon whose shoulders I stand for her guidance and favor; Maria Montessori for her audacity, her vision of peace and honoring of the child; my icon, Dr. Dorothy Irene Height for your blood, sweat, and tears for justice, for your inspiration, phenomenal womanhood, "hattitude," and because you are flat out "unmesswithable."

To Mr. Rich and Mrs. Nancy Kinder for your warmth and generosity; Mike Feinberg and Dave Levin for your outrageous, unprecedented gift and your tenacity; Catherine North, the consummate professional, for modeling the highest standard of excellence I have ever witnessed. What a role model you are for Sika (I want to be like you when I grow up).

To the teachers who have touched my life: L. P. Vaughn, Emma Wilson, Steve VanDyke Jackson, Leanna Williams, George Ellis, Dr. Elsie Lewis, Dr. Lynn K. Rhodes, Dr. Nancy Commins, Dr. Jawanza Kunjufu, Dr. Howard Fuller; my friend and the wind beneath my wings, the amazing Mary Ann Bash, for your encouragement and sisterhood, and for the archive in which you have chronicled my work for fifteen years.

To my cousin Norma Davis Felton for laughing at my stories and gently nudging me to write them down.

To my grandcat, Philadelphia, who is no longer with us but who thought she was a person for her sassiness, for sitting on my desk (sometimes keyboard), and for being my companion.

To the beautiful children I have guided who make me look so good in their shining lights. Thank you for your authenticity and all you have taught me. How wonderfully you have blessed my life with joy. To the parents of those children for your support and understanding when I forgot they were your children and acted as if they were my own; and for everyone else who has ever told me I was a wordsmith and that I could "lay it down on paper." I enfold you in my deepest love.

—Linda

# Table of Contents

# Foreword

At a time of stern assessments and restrictive practices levied upon the young, Linda Alston believes in the power of laughter and love. She welcomes the natural joy and playful spontaneity of childhood into her classroom and will not permit her own lively enthusiasms for the nobility of every child to be diminished in a fury of pedantry and paperwork.

"Once I teach the required lessons and teach them well," she states, "I allow the children the opportunity to think, build, imagine, explore, and express their creative genius." In other words, she lets them play. And furthermore, she gives herself permission to do the same, beginning with the fresh flowers she brings in daily to surround her inner-city children with the beauty and fragrance of the countryside. In Ms. Alston's room, child and teacher are free to become their best selves by exercising all their senses and using their intuitive knowledge, in tandem with new ideas, to build an intimate, happy learning community.

Today's child is sent off into a maze of schooling, starting with day-care and frequently thereafter pieced together between "before-school" and "after-school" segments. There seems little chance of discovering how one experience connects with the others. Do those who evaluate and label our children know them well enough to understand and appreciate their special qualities? If the school experience breaks down into lists of requirements and standards, how do we gain a true likeness of each child, and how will our children learn to know and trust themselves? Who will listen to our children's dreams and songs and find the narrative continuity that binds us together?

Linda Alston is not afraid to claim the responsibility. She is the bridge and bulwark between her students and their many worlds. In the clamor of everyday demands, she hears their unique voices and joins them in a communal search for answers to as yet unasked questions. As she moves to the rhythm and rhyme of the children, they learn to follow her lead into an exciting new school culture.

The classroom described in his book begins with each child and expands outward. The author's respect for the dignity of her children and their families is the linchpin of her philosophy, and the Golden Rule is her creed. *As I would have my say, I must allow the children to have theirs.*

*Why We Teach* is an honest and affectionately written memoir. It reaffirms our best reasons for becoming teachers. The magic is not to be found in any specific curriculum, but rather, in the spirit of optimistic expectation we bring into the classroom and our readiness to befriend and believe in each child. In demonstrating her own faith in the power of love and laughter in the lives of children, the author offers us new ways to retrieve and restore our faith in the art of teaching.

—Vivian Gussin Paley

# Preface

*"Thank you for participating in our Symposium on
Martin Luther King."*

Is this the welcome to the high school panel for the President's
Initiative on Race?

No, this is Amani, the 5-year-old master of ceremonies who invites
opinions and comments about Martin Luther King, Jr., from his kindergarten classmates who have studied the civil rights leader. In front of an
audience of 60 parents, Amani goes around and hands the microphone to
each student who offers an unscripted comment.

*"Shall I compare my mom to the moon? My mom is nicer
and more glowing."*

*"Shall I compare my little brother Elijah to the rain? He
is softer and more wet."*

Are these lines from a greeting card or a poetry reading?

No, these are the words of Anthony Nguyen and Jackson Aly,
5-year-old boys who are honoring their families in a Shakespearian style.

*"We cleaned up with alacrity so we could start our read-
ing and writing."*

Is this a think tank institute of doctoral scholars anxious to tackle
global problems? No, this is Uriel Villegas describing for me how and
why the children worked so quickly to clean up their table after a family-
style breakfast. They can't wait to read and write!

EXHIBIT A:

*Dear Room 129,*

*Pizza and ice cream sundaes? No way. This is not Pizza
Hut or Dairy Queen.*

*Adamantly,*

*The Principal*

Is this an internal memo at a corporate office?

No, this is evidence in the mock court case the Honorable Raymond
Jones heard in his courtroom about kindergartners who refused to read
and write beautiful stories unless their principal provided pizza and ice
cream. After all, in the book Ms. Alston read aloud to them, *Click, Clack,
Moo: Cows That Type,* the animals received electric blankets from the
farmer when they went on strike and withheld their milk and eggs! With
eye contact and respect, the 5-year-old witnesses answered Judge Jones's
probing questions with "Yes, Your Honor," and elaborated about their
read-aloud-inspired protest.

*"Thank you for your offer to tea, but I respectfully decline
so I can finish my 100s."*

Is this an invitation to High Tea at the Brown Palace, Denver's legendary salon named in honor of Molly Brown?

No, this is Ms. Alston's grace and courtesy curriculum in action.
When the children in Ms. Alston's room finish their work, they are welcome to invite a friend to have tea and a nutritious snack at the child-
size table set with china and a silver tea service. Of course, the tea patrons
must prepare the snack for themselves and clean up after their
tea so that others in the class may celebrate if they choose. And guests
are free to decline the invitation without offending the hosts.

*"Our first guest today is Estee Martinez, who will read the Pledge of Allegiance."*

Is this the beginning of a Town Hall meeting?

No, this is Noah Pacheco, the kindergarten co-host of Room 109's "Today Show," introducing a classmate who will lead one of the daily literacy activities. With undivided attention, Estee finds each word of the Pledge from a group of flashcards arranged randomly on a nearby table and places the flashcards in order in a pocket chart to read to the "television" audience. This is real reading with understanding of "allegiance," "republic," "indivisible," "liberty," and "justice." As Estee works in the background, the class's "Today Show" episode continues, featuring every student in the class, including Chef Jeremiah making pizza, Imani reading her favorite chapter from the venerable book *Owl at Home*, and Ruyee counting to ten in Chinese. Matt Lauer and Meredith Vieira have challengers in the wings!

When they arrive in August, 5-year-olds in Linda Alston's kindergarten class don't know about symposia, Shakespeare, synonyms, justice, Robert Frost, Desmund Tutu, Langston Hughes, Georgia O'Keeffe, or tea party etiquette. But in five short months they learn about these things and so much more. They learn to read excerpts from Martin Luther King, Jr.'s, "I Have a Dream" speech and to wash their silver tea service and china dishes gently and with confidence. Girls and boys learn to move around their beautiful, thoughtfully prepared classroom environment with grace and respect. They create art that is installed side-by-side with professional artists' work at an art gallery. They are learning one of life's most powerful lessons: "I can accomplish anything I work hard on and I am proud of my accomplishment." While child development psychologists explain that children achieve the ability to self-regulate their behavior between the ages of 4 and 8, Ms. Alston has developed such explicit and supportive guidance that all her 5-year-olds achieve remarkable levels of independence, which enables them to reach extraordinary levels of achievement.

While parents struggle to keep the children at their 5-year-old's birthday party in order, and coaches struggle to keep young players moving toward their goals on the soccer field, Ms. Alston seems omniscient. When a child reaches for food from a neighbor's plate at snack time, she gently guides him to ask for seconds politely. A child who tells a Native American guest singing in Lakota, "Your voice sounds funny," prompts Ms. Alston to lead a dialogue later about how it would make the children feel if someone said to them, "Oh, you sound funny!" She encourages them, "Maybe we can find a different word to describe something we're not used to hearing or seeing or tasting."

This IS the American dream . . . the conviction that education can give EVERY child equal opportunity. Linda's classroom is a place where young children learn to love one another, to honor their families, respect their community, challenge their minds, and discover their own gifts.

When children cross Linda Alston's threshold, they enter a world of fresh-cut flowers, silver tea services, appealing wooden learning materials, a sense of wonder, and a sense of order. Linda guides her students to become "their most magnificent selves" by helping to reveal the gifts within each of them. They find their gifts through song, dance, memorization, study, exploration, art, and storytelling. They emerge with poise, easily performing for and speaking to judges, elders, authors, small business owners, and corporate executives. Every day the children live their dreams, their freedom, their rights, and their responsibilities. Ms. Alston's work is transformational. She balances children's developing independence with the needs of the group, guiding the children to see themselves as responsible citizens. In an effort to combat an ethos of entitlement in a low-income community, she teaches her children and, through them, their families, to ask, "What can I contribute?" instead of "What can I get?"

Ms. Alston "lifts children out of poverty" through reading, writing, history, the arts, play, character building, grace, and belief in self. Linda's students—no matter what their backgrounds—have reached high levels of achievement because she adjusts her teaching to the unique needs and emerging interests of each new group of students.

—Mary Ann Bash, literacy specialist

"I leave you a thirst for education."
Dr. Mary McLeod Bethune

# It's in Every One of Us

ॐ

You are a teacher! Everyone teaches. Parents are their child's first teacher. Doctors teach us health and well being. Spiritual leaders teach us about the moral high ground and a power greater than ourselves. Bus drivers teach us to watch our step. Flight attendants teach us to put the oxygen mask over our mouths first and to breathe normally. Cable installers teach us how to navigate the technology they leave behind. Those who break the laws of society teach us through the consequences of their choices. Children teach us joy, trust, living in the moment, and unconditional love. And teachers, as professional educators from early childhood through high school, are the most magnificent of all. I bow to them.

These pages weave a rich and colorful tapestry of my journey as a public, private, charter, and Sunday school teacher. Each chapter tells a true story, as accurately as I can recall, about my life as a teacher and the joy and pathos that come with the territory. The stories span 40 glorious years and four states: Louisiana, Michigan, Wisconsin, and Colorado. At the beginning of each chapter are my own affirmations. I invite you to use these affirmations yourself because I affirm these ideals for all of us. At the end of each chapter is a reflection about what I learned from my various teaching experiences. You will also find questions to spark your own reflection.

You will love the children you meet in this book. Some live in project housing, homeless shelters for victims of domestic violence, or foster care. Others vacation in their families' privately owned mountain villas. No matter how wonderful and brilliant you already think children are, once you encounter the characters in this book, you will be brought up short. They have skin the color of licorice drops, creamy vanilla ice cream, the fruit of ripe bananas, crystallized ginger, cashews, and cocoa dust. Their ethnicities include African, African American, Caucasian, mixed race, Asian, Indigenous American Indian, and Latino/Hispanic. They range in age from 3 years old to 15. I have seen many of the students I taught as kindergartners go on to graduate high school and college, and to have children of their own. A wealth of them and their families remain an integral part of my life.

I made this book to be a delicious gumbo soup. While the pages contain a collection of real classroom stories, I hope that their messages will resonate with all who learn, laugh, love, and make a difference on the planet. Read the chapters in any order you choose. May you laugh until your cheeks hurt. May you cry a pool of tears. May those of you who teach outside of school settings come to see the teacher you truly are. And to my dear friends who are professional educators in our schools, may you see yourselves and your students in these events. I invite you to pack up your own treasure chest of enchanting experiences and ease on down the road with me toward a renewed understanding of, and appreciation for, why we teach.

Jeraldy serves tea and scones to our guest from Germany.

## Chapter One

# A Lovely Day

*"I am having a lovely and extraordinary day, this day!
Asé Asé!" (pronounced* ah-shay, *from the West African
Yoruba word meaning "amen")*

Teaching full-day kindergarten in an urban school with a student body
that is 98 percent "free and reduced lunch" brought with it harsh realities that no one should have to endure. In case you don't know, free and
reduced lunch means that the family of the child falls below a certain
income level. Located on Denver's near west side, the school mainly
serves children who live in the projects and a temporary housing unit
whose principle population is homeless survivors of domestic violence.

This is why I go the extra mile and beyond in an effort to make the children's day beautiful, safe, and consistent, or, as I like to say, "count-on-able," a word I made up that captures the stability my students need.

When the school day begins, I sit on a low chair by the door of my classroom to await the children. My classroom assistant brings the children in from the playground as the Bill Withers song "A Lovely Day" plays. I shake the hand of each child, call each of them by name, and say good morning. This ritual sets the tone of our day together. The music I choose is upbeat and happy. I also like "Here Comes the Sun" by the Beatles, "Pata Pata" by Miriam Mekeba, and "Ooh Child (Things Are Gonna Get Easier)" by Donnie McClurkin and Kirk Franklin. I don't just enter my classroom and wait to see how my day will unfold. I take charge and accept responsibility for thoughtfully organizing, initiating, and making sure everything, including our musical selection, is in place. The stage has now been set for our day to begin magnificently. The environment has been rigged for our highest achievement and success. We have been set up to win.

Order and beauty are very important in my classroom learning environment. I love plants, so I place them at the center of the work tables and along the windowsills, and I fill the room with beautiful baskets and artifacts that I have collected from all over the world. I also bring in fresh-cut flowers for the children to arrange and place around the classroom. I dust the shelves regularly and keep them neat and clutter-free. I think about how nice it feels to be in my own home when it is orderly, clean, and attractive. The children in my classroom enjoy this space of order and beauty as well. And, like home, the classroom gets cluttered and messy but the children and I always restore the room's balance and loveliness. Teachers and parents often remark that my classroom feels and looks like an attractive little home. We know we've created the right classroom environment when guests arrive and then find it hard to leave.

I teach kindergarten children how to serve tea to guests from a real silver tea service, complete with china that I purchased from a thrift store. The children wash, rinse, and dry the china dishware. Eric's grandfather, a master tailor, made cloth napkins for our class from African fabric that I brought back from Ghana. Before he stitched the sides of the napkins, Eric's grandfather sent me about 30 thread samples to choose from. Then he made sample napkins from my two choices, silver and gold. My final choice was the gold-colored thread. The children scrub the cloth napkins in small plastic dishpans with a scrub board and hang them on a drying rack to dry. The next day they fold the napkins. The children see a complete cycle, from a clean napkin to a soiled napkin to one that is washed, dried, folded, and placed back in the basket to be used again. Their participation in this process teaches the children to appreciate and respect the environment. They understand that by using the cloth napkins, instead of disposable ones, we are saving paper and trees.

I keep a guest book available so the people who visit our classroom can sign their names. It is nice to keep the guest books from years past. Some have signatures of people from all over the world and even include Chinese and Japanese characters. When people visit our school, one of the jobs on our classroom logistics team is that of docent, who requests that the guests sign the guest book.

At one school where I taught, we served breakfast in the classroom. The parents brought the children into the room, so each morning was a social gathering. It became important for me to establish clear boundaries and not get involved in discussing any one child in depth. But it made for a lovely period, when time allowed me to share wonderful stories about the children with their parents over breakfast. One morning I shared an anecdote with Rebecca and Mike, Robert's parents.

The children were practicing for a play that we would present at the end of the school year for the kindergarten continuation ceremony. In the script was the line, "Have you ever heard of Anansi the Spider?" This was one of Robert's lines. Except when Robert delivered it, he said, "Have you ever heard of Beyoncé the Spider?" The children and I cracked up laughing. It was one of those laugh-until-the-tears-flow kind of moments. Each time we came to the part of the play where Robert would say that line, everybody would lose it, and Robert loved making us laugh. Even after Robert learned how to say "Anansi the Spider" instead of "Beyoncé the Spider" everybody would still laugh from the memory. I finally edited it out of the play so that the show could go on. Rebecca and Mike loved the story and howled with laughter.

But morning sharing times could also bring frightening news; like the day Mike came in and told us about being shot during a robbery at his place of work. He gave a chilling account of how close he came to death. He showed me the newspaper article with his picture. And there was the morning when all the children were talking about the little baby girl who had died over the weekend in the temporary housing for victims of domestic violence across the street. Apparently the mother had gone out to the store to get cigarettes and left her baby in the bathtub.

After breakfast, my class gathers on the floor in a circle. I sit on the floor with them. I like the circle as opposed to the children sitting in rows and me sitting in a higher chair. The circle makes it possible for each of us to look into each other's eyes and faces so that when someone speaks, everyone can see him or her. The circle also creates positions of equality for each child and me. I do not consider myself superior to the children I teach or to any child. I am taller and I know more things, but that does not make me more important. When we sit in the circle, we all have a place of importance. The circle also allows the children to address their classmates and not direct their comments exclusively to the teacher. They can look around the circle and speak to everyone.

We start with a handshake and greeting. Each child shakes the hand of the child next to him or her and says good morning to that child, by name, until we come full circle. I like to change the greeting by using the word for "hello" in different languages. Sometimes we greet each other with "Jambo, Samantha" (Ki-Swahili), or "Ni hao, Eric" (Chinese), or "Bonjour, Joshua" (French), or "Hola, Mark" (Spanish).

We learn about the weather and the calendar and we discuss class business like upcoming field trips and the schedule of the day. I use every possible opportunity to infuse my language with rich vocabulary for the children. They acquire big words easily and effortlessly because they are immersed in them. In our classroom, we don't have just helpers. We have a Class Logistics Team. The jobs of the Logistics Team include the historian, who identifies the date on the calendar and any important upcoming events like assemblies, back to school night, or upcoming holidays; the meteorologist, who tells us about the weather for the day and what season it is (along with advice about proper dress to protect us from the elements); the facilitator, who reads the name and job of each child in order from the Logistics Team wall chart; the couriers, who messenger things to the office and bring papers back to us; the botanist, who waters our plants; the zoologist, who cares for the animals by feeding them and giving them water; the distributors and collectors, who pass out supplies; the custodians, who make sure we all clean up after ourselves and push our chairs under the tables; and the vision keeper, who reads our class-generated "vision" statement every day.

I create jobs on the Logistics Team as they become necessary. I make sure to give each job a title that sounds important and dignified. The children who put the chairs up on the tables at the end of the day are called chair technicians. One year I called them concierges. I write out job descriptions and send them home. The children must make a conscious choice to perform this duty. The receptionist, for example, receives a script of the proper phone greeting for our class, and takes it home to practice. When it is Shanique's turn to be the receptionist, she answers the phone, saying, "Good morning/afternoon, Ms. Alston's room, Shanique speaking, how may I assist you?" Or she might say, "Happy Springtime, Ms. Alston's room . . . ." The caller always lauds the receptionist for an excellent job answering the phone, which builds the child's confidence and self-esteem.

The positions on the Logistics Team rotate every week, so everyone has an opportunity to do each job. I teach the children that they are not "heir apparent" to the position of line leader. The word "leader" is an important and powerful one. When a child has the responsibility of being line leader, I teach him to model the proper behavior of a leader. Walk tall and straight, know where you are going, and walk in that direction, allowing no distractions. How they lead the line in kindergarten, I believe, is how they will achieve their goals in life . . . walking tall and straight with dignity and pride, knowing where they are going and not being distracted by the temptations of the world, seeing clearly their road and following it to success.

We review phonics from a chart on the wall, review sight words, vocabulary words, and then we sing. We love to sing. It is my hope that the day will never come when we are so busy as educators and so focused on test results that we don't have time for or value the importance of music, art, and movement. The children and I sing, clap, and rock that classroom. Singing songs with rhymes and playful lyrics provides a natural context for children to develop phonemic awareness. I teach a substantial part of a social studies lesson on the Reverend Dr. Martin Luther

King, Jr., slain civil rights leader, through song. We sing a song about Dr. King's dream—for everybody to love one another, enjoy the same freedoms, and let freedom ring—and we pledge to work together to make his dream come true. Yes, the children and I sing praises to the new day. Singing generates joy in the room and in our hearts, and I believe in the words of the great educator Loris Malaguzzi, "Nothing without Joy!"

The remainder of the morning is filled with reading and writing. Children work with differentiated materials on small rugs on the floor, read books independently, and write stories. It is during this time that I call children in groups of six to a table for guided reading. Each child has a copy of a text as we read and discuss the book. At the end of the morning we gather in the circle again. The children share their writings and their successes for that morning. I believe that it is important for students to own their education and to reflect in a metacognitive way about what they have learned. For example, a student might share that she is now leaving big "two finger" spaces between her words, which makes it easier for her and others to read her writing. Or another student might share that he found looking at the illustration in a book helped him comprehend what he was reading. After this gathering, it is time for lunch.

Following lunch, we have lessons in mathematics. After a full-group lesson, the children work individually and in small groups on the rugs on the floor. I encourage individual work during this time. If one child is working on a "100" board using tiles numbered from 1–100 and he completes it, I can do an "assessment at a glance." I note that the child has mastered that work and I record the information on a chart or in the child's assessment notebook. But if several students are doing a task together, I have no way of knowing who really knows what. I like to have each child master the work individually first, then they are free to work together as a team for reinforcement of the skill or task.

The afternoon is also the time for science, geography, and enrichment activities like plays and performances. We plant sunflower and buckwheat sprouts, said to be among the highest in nutritional value of any foods on the planet. We plant the sprouts in shallow trays filled with soil. Sometimes we call the sprouts "The Moveable Feast." When the children move on to first grade, they often come back to my classroom for some of my sprouts. If they visit at an inopportune time, I usually don't stop teaching my class and go cut sprouts for them. So I let them place their orders and I tell them what time to come back. When they return, I have their sprouts cut and packaged in plastic sandwich bags—healthy, fast food to go!

At the end of the day we come to the final circle. This is a time of celebration and reflection. Our days are always eventful—and often in most challenging ways. Maybe we heard a secret code word on the intercom telling us that we were "on lock down" and to hide behind Ms. Alston's desk, away from the windows; or perhaps the class witnessed two pregnant women fighting on the playground, and security was called. Or a parent came to pick up her child, wearing a shirt that reads, "Shit Happens When You Dance Naked." But for this moment, we are all safe and happy. We have broken bread, sung, danced, counted, read, written, and learned together. We write gratitude lists in our journals: "My friend played with me," "My friend helped me to tie my shoe," "We had strawberry milk for lunch," "I saw a big old hawk in that tree outside," "I wore my Spider Man shirt today," "I learned that I live in North America and that's a continent." And my gratitude lists are just as simple as the children's: "I saw a beautiful sunrise this morning," "I heard my favorite song on the radio," "I almost, but didn't slip on the ice," "Donavan knows all the sounds of the letters," "Emma can write her numbers from one to a thousand."

Sometimes we play the music of Kool and the Gang, "Celebrate." Or we dance to the music of the "Electric Slide." We never all go in the same direction and we bump into each other going and coming, but we don't care. We laugh, we celebrate, we embrace it all. It has been "a lovely day."

## REFLECTION

Children prosper in a beautifully balanced, clean learning environment, especially children whose homes lack order and consistency. I ask myself, "What can I do to make this a lovely and extraordinary day for the children?" What words might I use to encourage them? I will behold their individual gifts and talents. I will help each child to become his or her most magnificent self. I will learn the lessons that they are here to teach me . . . to laugh loud and play hard, to cry but not too long, when I fall down to pick myself up, brush myself off and get right back in the game, to eat only when I am hungry, to drink plenty of water, to love unconditionally, to let people know when they are not the boss of me, to take a nap when I am tired, to be in awe of everything, to wear my best clothes because I like how they look on me and not just when lots of people will see me, to sing and make up the lyrics as I go, to dance to my own rhythm, to love nature and life and magic and everything and to never stop learning.

As you think about the material in this chapter, ask yourself the following questions:

❦ Do you have a ritual for greeting children and starting the day in your classroom? Does what you do first thing in the morning help set a tone for the rest of the day?

❦ What do you do to create a pleasant environment for children in your classroom? Can you think of things you can do to beautify your classroom even more?

❦ Have you established a protocol for how students interact with visitors to the classroom? Can you think of other rituals you might add to ensure that students and your guests have a positive experience?

❦ Do you have adequate time built into your day for children to interact and share difficulties they may be having? Do you think your students view school as a safe place that inspires them to be the best people they can be?

The Milwaukee public school where I taught my first class.

## CHAPTER TWO

# Peter and the Po'k Chops

*"I trust my inner knowing."*

"Yo' funky bitch," Peter taunted the substitute teacher in his raspy voice. Then the second grader threatened to "snatch them gold chains off yo' neck." Peter was a gangbanger wannabe and the terror of the school. Even the fifth graders feared him. Most teachers avoided him at all costs; they had no idea how to deal with his out-of-control behavior. Peter had been retained, so he was bigger and older than the other second graders. He had threatened the substitute teacher when she had begged him to stop walking across the table and stepping with his muddy tennis shoes in each of the open books that the other children were trying to read. Three substitute teachers for this class had already quit, and I was observing the fourth so that I could take over the following day. After several years of working as a substitute teacher, I had been offered a full-time position in this first/second grade split classroom in inner-city Milwaukee.

While Peter was running rampant, the rest of the students were break dancing, fighting, screaming at each other, and throwing papers. I sat quietly in a chair in the corner near the teacher's desk, ready to duck under it if a child or an object came flying my way. I looked at a formation of desks near the wall. A little blonde girl named Rachel was laughing hysterically while three boys displayed angry snarls. I heard one boy say, "Ew, that's nasty, Rachel!" Rachel had told them that she was wearing no panties and that they could crawl under the desk and take a peek. But Rachel had a surprise for them. Once they were positioned under the table, she would pass gas aimed straight at their faces with all the force she could muster. The boys were upset by Rachel's master plan.

Let's just say it backfired on them.

I was terrified, and could not sleep that night. I wanted to run away from home, leave the state, and never look back. I felt scared to be in the same city with those children, not to mention in the classroom with them every day. No lesson plan or university course had prepared me for Peter, Rachel, and their associates. The other teachers kept their doors closed, they had no advice for me. The principal told me it was a very difficult class and wished me luck. What was I supposed to do the next day?

I had to retreat to an intuitive place inside myself to find the answers. What made sense to me was that I must disorient the students. My message must be clear that all the crazy behavior was over. I went in at six o'clock the next morning. I rearranged the desks into a semicircle.

I made pretty name-tag tents and placed them on each desk. From the couple of hours I observed the day before, I knew there were some students who should not be seated next to others. I put a tape into the cassette player. The music was "Spectrum Suite" by Steven Halpern. I knew that most of these students had probably never heard soothing, meditative music like this before. That was the whole idea. Disorient them. I placed lots of plants on the work tables. I scrubbed the room clean from top to bottom. There was order, balance, and beauty.

Now it was time to go and collect the children from the playground. The next idea that came from my intuitive place was to say few words. They were lined up in their place on the playground blacktop. As I approached, I could hear them whining, "Awwww, another substitute!" Others busted a little break dance move. They were happy to have fresh meat. I walked up to them poker-faced and said one word. "Come." I pivoted and walked briskly with confidence hoping that they were in tow. I never looked back. When I got to the classroom and checked, they were there, all 27. As was their custom, the students tried to barge into the room, yelling and cussing. I stopped them dead in their tracks. My next three words, in a very soft voice, were, "Single line here." Now I could hear some saying, "She crazy, she crazy, what she doin'?" I thought, good! I want them to think I'm crazy and unpredictable. They formed the line. They could hear the music and they had gotten a glimpse of the new classroom arrangement.

As each child entered, I shook his or her hand and said, "Good morning, it's a new day." I trusted they would have sense enough to go and sit at the desk where I had placed their name tent. They did. More questioning amongst themselves. "Why she got our desks like this?" They didn't ask me which I thought was interesting. Now I had to figure out what to say. I hadn't gotten that far yet. I explained to them that it was a new beginning. I said I knew of their reputation in the city, and I reminded them of what I had observed the day before. But, I assured these first and second graders that this was the last time I would speak of it. I would not hold them to their pasts. They were free to be redeemed and to begin again. "Some people believe that each day the whole world is born anew," I told them. "You have a chance to make a new beginning with me."

By lunchtime, teachers were coming to the door and looking in with amazement. They would get other teachers to come behold the miracle. They were saying, "What did she do to these children? She speaks so softly, she didn't even raise her voice!" The principal called the administrators at the central office and told them they had to come and see the difference with those children in one morning.

Reading this, you may be saying, "So what did you do? Did I miss something? It can't be that simple!" I submit to you that it can. What I did was very simple. I believed in myself. I believed in the children. And I trusted my own answers and had faith that what I was doing would work. The answers lie in one's fundamental beliefs about children. I had to go down deep and get back in touch with those beliefs. I love children. I believe that children are good. I believe that children love learning. They want to be safe and happy and engaged in thinking and learning about themselves and the world around them. What I had witnessed the day before clashed with those beliefs. I had to create a mental image and tap into a visceral understanding of who I knew children to be. I had to stand in knowing the truth about children. They are beautiful creations who want to be children.

The four substitutes had spent too much time in the valley of fear. You might wonder what would have happened if the children had not come with me from the playground or lined up outside the door. Here is my answer. I would have trusted my intuition to try THE NEXT BEST

THING! But I would have continued to stand firm in my belief that this must work. I intended to make it work, so it must work. These were poor children with hard lives. Their futures were at stake. There was no back door! I couldn't give myself over to the anxiety so easy to experience when confronted with misbehaving children, impossible parents, unreasonable administrators, and the lack of resources as basic as paper and pencils. But if you make up your mind that you will be triumphant, you will be. Trust that you know what will work.

My class had not been invited to the Christmas program because of the terrible behavior that had driven four substitute teachers from the school. I decided not to push the matter. I had only been their teacher since November. But I promised them that I would not allow them to be excluded from anything else at school that year. After the Christmas break, we got busy. The next event was Black History Month and the Black History Contest. The students all studied hard. Each morning the secretary would read a question about black history over the intercom. Each class had only a few minutes to write down the answer. We would collect them and a runner would take them to the office. The class with the most correct answers would win. My class won almost every day. At the end of the month, we were declared the champions, and I treated the children to a soul food luncheon in the classroom.

The next school-wide competition was the spelling contest. My little Myseha won it with room to spare. I asked her what she wanted as her celebration gift from me. She said she wanted me to cook shrimp for her in the classroom and for us to have lunch in the classroom as we did for the Black History luncheon, except that she would like to invite some of her friends, and no boys could attend. I agreed. I brought in my electric frying pan. We had that whole school smelling like Red Lobster. We were frying up those shrimp.

Finally came the day of the mathematics competition. There was no question in any of our minds about whom we should groom to represent us in that contest. It was Peter. Peter was a brilliant mathematician. Before I arrived, Peter would miss a lot of school. He would hang out at the neighborhood grocery store, carrying people's groceries or returning their shopping cart for pocket change. To this day, I wonder why nobody, especially the store manager, cared enough to alert the school that a child was spending his days at the store instead of school. But this was how Peter learned how to count money. He excelled in math in my class. I even let Peter balance my checkbook. I would ask him to add up all these numbers, subtract this total from the balance, and tell me what he got as an answer. He would always get it right. Peter could do the math, and I trusted him, so Peter was the one.

On the day of the math contest in May, Peter wore a white T-shirt with hot pink, raised velvet letters that read, "Ms. Lovemaker," which was obviously his mother's. When I asked him why he chose that shirt, he told me it was the only shirt he could find in his house that was clean. I tried calling Peter's house to see if his mother would bring him another shirt. A man's voice answered. I identified myself and asked for the shirt. The response was, "Peter say you pretty and you got braids and you nice. What else you do besides teach school?" I slammed the phone down and went back to the classroom.

Fortunately, that day I had worn a white oxford shirt and a school T-shirt on top. I took off my school shirt and gave it to Peter to wear. He was worthy of so much more. Our class went to the auditorium for the math contest. Peter won. I had already asked Peter what he wanted for his treat because I knew he would win. He had worked hard and was prepared. He said he wanted me to cook pork chops in the classroom for him and he wanted to invite some of his "boys." When Peter won, we all stood up and cheered for him. His silly grin lit up the auditorium. He looked out at me and mouthed as he held his fist high in victory, "po'k chops, po'k chops, po'k chops."

## REFLECTION

There will never be enough teachers' manuals or courses to answer all the situations we face as teachers. The outside experts have not been in our classrooms. They do not know our children. We must learn to rely on our intuition and be confident that it will work.

As you think about the material in this chapter, ask yourself the following questions:

- What are some of my fundamental beliefs about children? How do these beliefs affect my teaching?

- What challenging situations am I currently facing in my classroom?

- How can I use my intuitive understanding of my students to address these situations?

- What are some out-of-the-box solutions I have used in the past? What are some that I can use now?

To this day, Christian's worm-in-green-slime bottle adorns my desk.

## CHAPTER THREE

# Who Put the Worm in Green Slime on My Desk?

*"I choose to be inspired by experiences I first judged to be uninspiring."*

"I'm really sorry, but our budget has been cut and one of you will be out of a job." The principal was visibly saddened by this latest development at our preschool-through-eighth grade charter school in Denver, Colorado. I had been teaching a full-day kindergarten class there for only one year. The two other kindergarten teachers and I sat listening to her words barely breathing. There were three teachers and two jobs, a mathematical word problem our kindergarten students could figure out. "The three of you need to come to my office at two o'clock this afternoon so we can figure out what we will do."

A kind of comic relief comes over me at the strangest times, a peculiar humor that often only I think is funny. I knew there were very good odds (another mathematical concept I had recently introduced to my kindergarten class) that I would be the one to get the pink slip. Having taught the least number of years at this school, I was on shaky ground. But I had an idea. I proposed to the other two teachers that we get some red cellophane to resemble fire, and brown construction paper to make a torch. At two o'clock we march upstairs to the principal's office with our torches, humming the "Survivor" theme, and find out who gets their torch snuffed and voted off the "island." My esteemed colleagues did not find that notion one bit funny and declined my request. We ascended the impressive staircase, which still had the original carved wood spindles, torchless.

When the three of us reached the principal's office, she proposed another option. One of us could move up to middle school and teach language arts to the sixth, seventh, and eighth graders. The principal and other administrators implored me to stay and assured me of how masterful I would be in this position. I thought about it. I did love literature with a deep passion. The curriculum included some of my favorite writers, like Robert Frost, Langston Hughes, Alex Haley, and Maya Angelou. I thought maybe a change might be just what I needed. I could get away from those little kindergartners for a while. This decision would be a win for everybody, especially the middle school students who would be so fortunate to have me as their language arts teacher. I envisioned them hanging on my every word as I uttered eloquent profundities for them to ponder. I couldn't have been further from the truth.

It is a joy to work with teachers. They are a fascinating group of dedicated professionals. Many teachers have a proclivity for a certain grade level. And I don't mean elementary school, middle school, high school, or college. I am talking about eleventh grade, sixth grade, second grade, or kindergarten—specific grades. Teachers can explain in copious detail why their grade is "all that and a cowry shell." A friend who teaches second graders adores that age group because she says they are not as whiny as first graders and are more settled in and ready to learn. She says second graders have knowledge that she can build upon. Some teachers enjoy the rambunctious personalities of eighth graders. Teachers can list all the redeeming qualities of the grade they teach and will defend those students like a lioness would her cubs.

When I moved up to my new middle school adventure, away from my "pweshiss yittle kindergarten babies" (I tend to revert back to baby talk when thinking about them, but would never speak that way to them directly), I was curious to discover what I would like about these students. The sixth-, seventh-, and eighth-grade students were physically bigger, of course, but I soon learned that they were still little children who loved unconditionally and while their raging hormones made them act quite silly, they wanted to learn.

An open mind was what I needed to get to know my new students. The classroom environment needed to reflect my respect for their maturity. The students knew that I had taught kindergarten at the school the year before. The room had to be beautiful and engaging. That was my forte. I couldn't have it any other way. But the room also had to be appropriate for middle-school students. A friend helped me hang posters of famous landmarks from around the world, striking pictures of the Eiffel Tower, the Great Wall of China, the Taj Mahal, the pyramids of Egypt, and the Golden Gate Bridge, lending beauty and sophistication to the classroom walls. Art pieces and cloth from different parts of the world alternated with green plants along the window ledge. Globes, atlases, dictionaries and a few computers stood at the ready. The classroom was clean, organized, and attractive. Bring on the students, I thought to myself.

The building lacked an electronic bell system, so a teacher had to leave the classroom and walk out into the hall in order to ring an old-fashioned gold bell with a dark wooden handle. The sound of the bell signaled the students to change classes. My first class was the sixth graders. They had written letters to me welcoming me to middle school. One of the letters told me not to be scared. There were about 28 students total. All were special and interesting in their own unique way, just as I had imagined. Though I had my work cut out for me academically (their writing was comparable to that of my kindergartners), the sixth grade students worked hard, and we all got along fine from the start.

The seventh and eighth grade classes were another story. Except for about seven of them, none of the students wanted to work in my class-room. The handful of students who were cooperating sat in the front row of desks and strained to hear what I was trying to teach, while the rest of them sat at two large work tables in the back of the classroom. The boys went to the table on the left and the girls went to the table on the right. The boys played a game called "Bloody Knuckles." Two boys would spin a quarter at the same time, and the boy whose quarter kept spinning the longest was the winner. The loser had to allow the winner to take his quarter and strike it across his knuckles as hard as he could until the loser's knuckles bled. Meanwhile, the girls sat at their own table, applying lip gloss and polishing their fingernails. I tried pleading with these students to participate in class. I called parents. The principal came in and talked to them. As soon as she walked out of the classroom door, they went right back to "Bloody Knuckles" and cosmetology.

It was devastating for me to watch these students waste their time and fritter their lives away. Each day the same seven students sat in the front doing their work while the behavior of the rest of the class spiraled downhill. The students at the back tables started to throw pencils and markers. The harder I tried to get them to participate in our class work, the more hostile they became. I felt my back was against the wall. My high expectations, clear boundaries, and beautiful learning environment were not cutting it here. I had to go further. Again, I called parents and asked for help from the principal. I begged and pleaded. I even considered instituting a reward system in which the students could earn points toward prizes for good behavior and completing their work. Philosophically, I do not believe in rewarding students by giving a token for every little thing they do, as if I'm throwing fish to the dolphins. Celebrating major accomplishments makes sense, but bribing students makes me feel like I'm being held hostage in my own classroom. I knew that if I could get the students to experience that indescribable feeling of intrinsic validation and success that comes from deep within, it would be the greatest gift I could give them. Once a student develops a hunger and thirst for knowledge and a desire for excellence, no one can take it away.

After a few weeks, I asked the custodians to remove the two round tables from the classroom. On that day, the students came into the classroom and found all the desks in a big circle. With no tables in the classroom, the Bloody Knuckles boys and the lip-gloss girls didn't have anywhere to set up their operations. They were caught off guard and so they angrily threw themselves into the chairs. There is something sacred and compelling about a circle. The students wanted to move the desks, but somehow our circle remained unbroken.

I read aloud from Mary Shelley's *Frankenstein*. The author describes how Dr. Victor Frankenstein creates this ugly creature in his laboratory and how the monster runs away to hide in the mountains of the Swiss

Alps. When Dr. Frankenstein and the monster reunite, the monster Frankenstein pours out his soul to his creator, telling him how sad he is. He has no friends, family, or property, and has never had a father to play with him or a mother to love and smile at him. No one will come near him because of his scary appearance. He says that he has never seen anyone else who resembles him. The passage ends with, "The question that comes to me again and again through my groans is: What am I?" I read that passage with all the empathy and inflection I could evoke.

When I raised my eyes from the book, many of these bad-to-the-bone seventh- and eighth-grade boys were sniffing and trying to hide their emotions. The lip-gloss girls' mascara started to run in black streaks down their faces. They cried and giggled at the same time. One girl got up from the circle and got a box of tissues from my desk. She pulled three tissues from the box in rapid jerks, blew her nose, and passed the box to the girl next to her. The students avoided each other's eyes so as not to risk revealing an emotional response. I had done my part. I had read the story aloud to them. I was no longer the teacher and facilitator, but another member of the discussion group. Finally, one girl said, "He musta been scared and cold and he didn't have no mama." One of the "Bloody Knuckles boys" said, "Daaaaaaaang." The brass-handle bell sounded in the hall and the students filed out of my room.

The next day in class those seventh- and eighth-grade students wrote responses to the Frankenstein passage that were three and four pages long. Before this assignment, the most I could ever get them to write were short answers in a fill-in-the-blanks lesson sheet. We had days and days of editing ahead of us, however. Their handwriting, grammar, spelling, and punctuation were atrocious, but their ideas were good. They made connections between the text and their own lives, such as writing about times when they were scared and nobody wanted to be their friend. One boy named Samuel started teasing another boy, Juan, about how the story had made Juan cry and a fight almost broke out between the two of them. One of the lip-gloss girls, Estephanie, told the boys, "Why don't y'all sit down somewhere so we could finish our work, 'cause we trying to learn somethin' up in here, huh Ms. Alston?" Their behavior after that was far from perfect, but at least I had reached them, and they knew what it felt like to be engaged in their own learning.

I thought maybe a compromise between giving the students individual rewards for making progress and nothing at all would be to get something nice for all the classes to share. But what could that be? I happened to be attending a meeting near a gift shop that was located many miles away from my home. The business was closed but it was not hard to spot the seven-foot foil Frankenstein balloon inside. I knew that balloon would make an awesome addition to the classroom and add interest to our *Frankenstein* writings. Plus, it was almost time for Halloween.

I jotted down the name of the gift shop and called the number a few days later to inquire about the balloon. The store owner said that it was the last one they had but that I could purchase it for $29.95. I really wanted that balloon for my students, but I didn't want to drive all the way back out there and I didn't want to pay that much for it. One day I mentioned to the students that I had seen the balloon and how cool it was. I asked if they thought I should drive all those miles to get it for them. Carlos said, "Ms. Alston, my auntie works for a balloon store. I know that balloon you talkin' 'bout. I seen it. I'll ask my auntie to get us one for free." As promised, the next day Carlos came to school with the seven-foot Frankenstein balloon. He had to leave it in a storage room until it was time to bring it to class. It caused quite a commotion at the school. We kept Frankenstein inside the classroom during class, but when the brass bell rang, we let him float out in the hallway, tethered to a doorstop so the students could see him as they changed classes. We were happy that Frankenstein now had all these friends who loved him and thought he was "the bomb." My sixth graders loved him, too. They punched him gently and laughed and played with Frankenstein. He had many new friends and was not lonely anymore.

When the students returned to my class the next day they seemed appreciative that Carlos had brought it. It had been fun, and maybe now they would settle down more and focus on their work. But according to our schedule, this day was the day for me to take the class to the computer lab to learn technology.

The technology teacher taught the lessons, and my role in the computer lab was to assist the technician and redirect the students. My seventh- and eighth-grade class had finished their computer lesson early and we had about ten minutes left. We hadn't planned anything for this down time, but an idea occurred to me to ask the students to write down the months of the year on a sheet of paper as a little spelling pop quiz. Only a few of the students spelled all the months correctly. One boy spelled the month of August, "ogiss." When we got back to the classroom, I told them that I was disappointed that everyone did not get 100 percent on the quiz. I said, "As seventh and eighth graders, you should know how to spell the days of the week and months of the year." I didn't mean to insult them, but that is what happened. Their shame came out in the form of rage. One boy flipped a desk over. "That wasn't our lesson no way," he protested. "We was in computer. You ain't told us we had to know that." I felt as if all we had gained was lost again. I was back at square one. One of the lip-gloss girls left an anonymous note calling me a "bicth." The spelling of "ogiss" and "bicth," and all the editing we had to do with their papers made me realize how far behind these students were and how much work it was going to take for them to catch up.

Earlier, when I thought I was going to be the teacher to get voted off the island, I had made a couple of inquiries about jobs at other schools. I find that dramatic life events and circumstances tend to come in waves. One day, two different principals called and offered me jobs. The first offer was for a position teaching an early childhood, preschool class and the other was a first-grade class. At this point, I felt I had made some progress with these middle school students, but I decided that a strong middle school teacher would serve them better. Tyler Perry's character Medea would have been a good candidate for the job. You have to know when to hold them and when to fold them. It was time to fold. I accepted the first-grade teaching position. I wanted to be as close as I could to the grade level I loved best, kindergarten, so that I could continue to give students the kind of foundation necessary to prevent such an enormous achievement gap.

The month was now November. The students learned that I was leaving before I'd had the opportunity to tell them myself. My sixth graders were very sad to see me leave. The seventh and eighth graders said, "Whatever!" On my last day, I walked into my classroom and saw a green, plastic bottle sitting on my desk. My name, Ms. Linda Alston, had been written on it in black, permanent marker. When I looked at it closely, I realized that the bottle was filled with green slime, with a white plastic worm floating around in it. I slumped down into my chair and started to cry. This whole middle school experience had been a big, fat fiasco. The students had summarized how they felt about me as their teacher with this gift: "Green Slime With White Worm," an artistic still life.

A grandmother's voice startled me out of my sorrowful abyss. "I heard you were leaving. He gave you that?" I realized that it was Christian's grandmother. Before I could ask her whom she was talking about, she continued. "I can't believe Christian gave you that slime bottle. He made that in science class last year. That's his prize possession. He must really love you, Ms. Alston. We are sorry to see you go. You were doing a good job with these kids . . . makin' 'em learn." She turned and walked out of the classroom murmuring to herself . . . "Um, um, um, he gave her that slime bottle. I can't believe it."

## REFLECTION

The green slime worm bottle has become a metaphor for me. It reminds me not to attach meaning to an object or situation without really knowing the reality. One boy's slime bottle can be a teacher's trophy of love and appreciation—something to keep on her desk for years to come. The gift from Christian taught me that even though a situation might seem unpleasant at first, if I give it time, I will discover its value in my life.

As you think about the material in this chapter, ask yourself the following questions:

- Do you have your own "worm in green slime" story? Describe a time when you misinterpreted the comments or actions of one of your students.

- How have you turned challenging situations in your classroom into inspiring learning opportunities?

- In what ways have you used humor at school to diffuse tension and difficulties?

- What have you done to motivate your students to get excited about learning? How do you feel about extrinsic rewards for achievement, such as awarding points and prizes?

Fresh anthuriums arrived by express mail from
Hilo, Hawaii, for our kindergarten graduation.

## CHAPTER FOUR

# From Community Helpers
# to the Big Island

*"My community is rich with humanity and history and
my heart listens to its story."*

જી

It was a Saturday morning in July 2001 and the marketplace was
bustling. The wooden kiosks strained under the weight of pineapples,
mangos, beads, cloth, carvings, and jewels. Using the dye of the henna
plant, the artist painted designs on my arms with meticulous care. I
dropped my head back, closed my eyes, and let my body sink deeper into
the lawn chair. Smells of flowers and fresh fish competed with each other.

"How is it that you like our island?" the artist asked without lifting
her eyes from her intricate creation on my left arm. "It is a paradise," I

said as I reflected on how I had come to be here in Hawaii. The whole series of events still seemed surreal. Just when I think life can't get any better, it flat out does. I am a living example that when you do what you truly love—in my case teaching—life will serve you up gifts beyond your wildest imaginings. How could I have ever dreamed that teaching a unit on community helpers would lead me to paradise in Hilo, Hawaii?

In kindergarten, a portion of the social studies curriculum is routinely dedicated to the study of community helpers. In my effort to make learning fun and exciting for the children, I think of ways for them to experience the real world outside the classroom. I avoid the predictable and mundane. Each lesson and unit of study is as true to life as possible. Instead of buying traditional community helper cartoon character pictures and mounting them on the walls, we plunged into our community and experienced it firsthand. And if ever there was a community that was rich in history and heroic figures, the Northeast Denver area surrounding the Wyatt-Edison Charter School was the one.

In my second year of teaching full-day kindergarten at the charter school, I began a unit of study on community helpers. My plan depended a great deal on the participation of classroom parents, so I wanted to establish a relationship of trust, comfort, and approachability from the first day of school. Instead of sending home a questionnaire, I decided that informal, personal interaction would be much more effective. I asked them about themselves: what kind of work they did, their hobbies, their talents and life experiences, and established a rapport. This way, when I told them one morning that we were beginning a unit of study on community helpers, they weren't taken by surprise when I asked them if they would help out. Most were willing to schedule a time to come in and discuss their lives with the class. I then initiated a conversation with the students to elicit their thoughts about the community: what they liked and did not like, what activities they enjoyed, and what places they had visited.

Cynthia was a 5-year-old Hispanic child with a very pleasant personality. Like many other kindergartners, she was missing her front teeth. It seemed that as the other kindergartners' permanent teeth began to grow in, Cynthia's never would. But that did not stop Cynthia from smiling all the time and licking her tongue in the space frequently to check for any sign of new teeth breaking through her gums. During my introductory lesson about community helpers, Cynthia told us that her grandpa owned a bakery close to our school. The children and I were so excited to learn this information. When Cynthia's cousin came to pick her up from school at the end of the day, I asked him where the bakery was located. He gave me the address, and the next day we walked about three blocks up the street to the business. Cynthia's grandpa didn't speak very much English, but Cynthia showed us around and smiled her toothless smile and we smiled, too, and said "muchas gracias" when we left. Cynthia felt very proud to share her grandpa's bakery with us.

One day a teacher at the school introduced me to Sister Jean and told me about her Sharing and Caring Ministry. Sister Jean was an African-American woman who, along with her husband, Michael (a retired teacher who had taught in the Denver public schools for 30 years), had established a chapel, computer lab, food and clothing bank, and other emergency services for our community. The Sharing and Caring Ministries would be our next field trip. This was another great service in our community within walking distance from the school, and Sister Jean and Michael were certainly community helpers to learn about and appreciate.

On a bright sunny day the children and I walked through our beautiful neighborhood to visit Sister Jean. As we walked we admired the flowers around the houses. We passed by an old historic church and gazed up in awe at the splendid architecture. There was a quatrefoil shape at the top of a window beneath the steeple. Ajannae was quick to take notice of this shape and point it out to the rest of us. She remembered this shape from our geometry study in the classroom and had now recognized it out in the world. This was very exciting.

Sister Jean greeted us warmly and gave us a tour of the center. Some of the children remembered that they had come to Sharing and Caring Ministries to get food for their families. The clothes and food banks were well organized. The clothing area looked more like a department store where you would buy new clothing. The blouses, pants, and coats hung neatly on the hangers and were color coordinated. There was no "used clothes smell" typical of secondhand stores. The air was fresh and clean. The same was true for the food bank. All the cans, boxes, and bags were lined up on the shelves, with no accumulation of dust on the tops. Sister Jean's love and generosity filled the space. At the end of the tour, she gave each child a special can of chili labeled with a Denver Broncos' sticker. The children expressed their excitement and gratitude.

We walked back to the school having learned about two more community helpers. We invited Sister Jean to visit our classroom, and she cried when she heard the children sing "My Life Is in Your Hands" by Kirk Franklin. The children gave her canned goods for her food bank. This was an opportunity to teach the children that life is not just about what we get, but about what we give. It was a small effort to strike down attitudes of entitlement and hopelessness that are sometimes entrenched in high-poverty areas—and instill in the children a feeling that they have something to offer others.

One of my favorite affirmations is "Everything I do turns out better than I planned it." What began as a social studies unit about community helpers to meet the state standards, continued for the entire school year. We learned about the rich history and heritage of our school community, all within a five-mile radius. Another community member who lightened our hearts and taught us so much was Daddy Bruce Randolph, a man with the face of an angel and a heart as big as the cerulean Denver sky.

Daddy Bruce, as he was lovingly called, opened the Barbeque Restaurant in the Five Points neighborhood when he was 61 years old. He believed that no one should go hungry anytime, but especially not on Thanksgiving Day, when Americans celebrate abundance and give thanks for all their blessings around a huge dinner table. On Thanksgiving Day, Daddy Bruce began a tradition of serving at his restaurant a traditional turkey dinner with all the trimmings, free of charge, to poor and disadvantaged people of all races. In the beginning, Daddy Bruce fed people with his own money. When the project became more than Daddy Bruce could afford, professional athletes, politicians, firefighters, police officers, nuns, clergy, and citizens from every walk of life volunteered resources and time to cook and serve the hungry. Daddy Bruce lived to see the street where his restaurant stands named in his honor. A middle school was also named for this great humanitarian. When asked why he fed thousands of people on Thanksgiving, Daddy Bruce responded, "You can't beat love. Nothing beats love. If you give just one thing, you get three things back. That's why I do it."

The children and I walked to Daddy Bruce's restaurant. We stood outside and enjoyed the smell of sizzling ribs and smoky barbeque sauce. We took away not only the joy of good food, but a life lesson, too. Learning about this man taught the children that it is noble to give and that you don't have to be a rich and famous person to be generous.

The Black America West Museum and Heritage Center was once the home of Dr. Justina Ford. This charming, Victorian building is an historic landmark and located just a few blocks from our school. In 1950, Dr. Ford was the first physician in Colorado to be both African American and female. She specialized in gynecology, obstetrics, and pediatrics. Her husband, Reverend John L. Ford, was a minister in Denver. Dr. Justina Ford is said to have delivered over seven thousand babies to underprivileged people in the community. Some histories report that Dr. Ford donated a large portion of her earnings back to the community for young people to attend college. Near the end of her life of extraordinary service, she was quoted as saying, "When all the fears, hate, and even some death is over, we will really be brothers. . . . This I believe. For this I have worked all my life."

Our class visit to the home of Dr. Justina instilled some important lessons. The children learned that girls can be doctors and that when you become educated and successful, you don't have to leave your community. You can stay and help others.

Our school was housed in the century-old historic Wyatt School building, which was owned by the Phillips Foundation. Mr. Charles "Chuck" Phillips, chairman and CEO, came to Denver in 1953 at the age of 17 with 30 cents in his pocket. For a time, he was homeless and survived by doing odd jobs, but eventually became a financial success and living legend by working in real estate, auto bodywork, construction, and other business ventures. In 1996, Mr. Phillips renovated the school building. He "adopted" our kindergarten class and became a loving grandfather-like role model for the children. He would often pop into the classroom unannounced. The children would run to him and give him hugs. Then they would want to share all the things they were studying and reading about with him or they would want to sing to their hero. Sometimes he would ask me, "Linda, how many of my babies are in this room?" My answer would be anywhere from 20 to 25. He would then go out and get pizza or ice cream and surprise us with a treat, the same way he surprised me with a catfish dinner the day Ms. Flo had the fish fry behind the school.

Ms. Flo was one of the most colorful characters at the school. The grandmother of several students, Ms. Flo volunteered often and did not hesitate to speak her mind about anything that she did not agree with regarding the ways in which the school was being operated. Making copies of work for the children in different classes and grade levels was Ms. Flo's main job. One day, when the copying machine broke down, Ms. Flo did not wait around for it to be repaired. She had work to do. The next thing we knew, Ms. Flo was behind the school on the sidewalk with a cooking setup frying catfish and barbequing ribs. Around lunchtime, I could smell the aromas of the fish and ribs. I went out back and said, "Ms. Flo, what on earth are you doing?" Her answer was, "What does it look like I'm doing? I'm selling dinners." I said, "It looks good; I'll have a catfish dinner. Give me a minute to go back into the classroom and get the money." Ms. Flo said, "Don't worry about it, Mr. Phillips got you covered. He done already paid for yours." Afterward, she donated the money to buy a new copier.

Ms. Flo was generous in other ways, too. She enjoyed sharing with the students of the school her old artifacts from the past. She owned an impressive collection of antiques including scrub boards, smoothing irons, embroidered linens, and her favorite treasure, the "slop jar." Ms. Flo would make the students howl with laughter when she told them about the days before people had indoor plumbing and bathrooms, when they had to use the "slop jar" at night. She made sure that when the students filed by her carefully organized display in the foyer, the "slop jar" did not escape their notice.

Codisha's grandfather, Mr. Frank "Sonny Boy" Terry picked his granddaughter up from school at the end of the day. He was very patient and did not mind waiting as Codisha did math problems on the white board. Although we had a longer school year, which extended into July, and a longer school day, which ended at four o' clock, Codisha was never quite ready to leave her kindergarten classroom. Mr. Frank and I would talk while he waited for Codisha to finish. In one of our conversations, Mr. Frank shared with me that he had his own blues band. Well, before he could get the sentence out of his mouth, I had booked him and his band to play for our class Christmas party.

The holiday menu consisted of a submarine sandwich that spanned an entire worktable, chips, cookies, vegetables, and punch. I did not inform the parents that we were having entertainment, just in case Mr. Frank had to cancel. When they arrived for the party at about one o'clock in the afternoon, they were pleasantly surprised to hear Mr. Frank and his band belting out "The Thrill Is Gone" by B. B. King. Some parents were having such a good time that they called their places of employment and took the rest of the afternoon off. The parents said they didn't know that a kindergarten party could be so much fun. People were actually dancing in the classroom. The children danced and enjoyed seeing the adults having so much fun. Mr. Frank and his band volunteered a few more times during the school year. Our class might have been the only kindergarten class in history to have had its own blues band, on call and at the ready to perform.

Parents came to our classroom to share not just their careers but their lives. Ian's father was from Japan. Ian's mother cooked Japanese food for us. I explained to the parents that there was no need to make a big production of their sharing. Whatever they had to say was welcomed and appreciated. Almost 50 percent of the parents came to the classroom and talked about their work and themselves. We enjoyed learning from a student in a Women's Studies Program at the University, a nurse, a sheriff, a cosmetologist, a mother with a talking parrot, and a minister. On a daily basis, parents could be found in my classroom, inviting the children to read to them, working on art projects, and having grand fun.

The day I asked Kiana's grandfather, Wally, what he did for a living is a day I shall long remember. He told me that he worked with decals. Of course I invited him back to share some of his work with the class. He returned a few days later with a huge collection of decals to show us. Wally gave all the children some of their favorite decals to take home. He thanked me for teaching his granddaughter Kiana so much. Wally went on to mention that he and his wife, Pam, were building a home and retiring to Hilo, Hawaii. He invited me to visit them in Hawaii and told me that I would have the honor of being the very first person to stay in their guest quarters. I thought that he was being sweet, but did not really take him seriously. Kiana had been writing stories in class about how she was going to visit her grandma and grandpa in Hawaii in the summer. Wally, Pam, and Kiana's mother, Briana, continued to ask me to come to Hawaii. Kiana's grandparents left for Hilo some time in February. They sent me e-mails with pictures of how beautiful the island was and where they were planning to take me when I came. Kiana's "papa" said that when the volcanoes erupted, the hot lava would run in streams in certain areas. Wally said that when I came to Hawaii, we would all go on a picnic beside the lava flow. He explained that we would wrap a prime rib roast in ti leaves and bury it in the molten hot lava in a hole in the ground. The heat would cook the roast, and we would eat it together with the other food we brought along. I thought it all sounded pretty exotic. I had not planned to go to Hawaii that summer, but with every e-mail that arrived, the invitation sounded better and better.

As the end of the year came, the children and I planned a continuation ceremony. I have vacillated back and forth over the concept of a kindergarten graduation. Some assert that it is much ado about little. After all, they are only completing kindergarten. They argue that it will take away from the big one—high school graduation. But I came to embrace the idea and opted for a full-blown ritual, complete with caps and gowns. I came to this decision because of the nature of the communities in which I have chosen to teach. Most have been plagued with crime, drugs, gang violence, and teen pregnancy. Some of these children might not live to see their high school graduation. Some might have babies and complete high school with a GED, if they are persistent. I hold my students high and call forth their highest good, always. But this is the grim reality. Many of their parents faced difficult situations daily just trying to survive. So, why not just celebrate this one year of success by having a formal ceremony to encourage the children and delight their parents?

This much I know is true: When they graduate from high school, children can't possibly look as adorable as they do as kindergartners. That year, the children chose white caps and gowns with baby blue tassels. On the day before the ceremony, I received a huge box that had been express-mailed from Hilo, Hawaii. It contained 25 fresh leis made of plumeria and other native flowers. Also carefully packed inside the box was a bouquet of red, pink, and white anthuriums for me.

On the evening of the continuation, the parents packed the auditorium. With the lights dimmed, the children marched slowly up the center aisle, each holding a battery-lit candle, and dressed in their white caps and gowns with the baby blue tassels as the song "It's in Every One of Us" played. One by one, students stood at the microphone and read an original reflection about what they had learned in kindergarten. Mr. Phillips and his family were there. Ms. Flo was there, serving refreshments for us and orchestrating everything to make sure it turned out just right.

July found me eating fresh papaya for breakfast every morning, hiking through orchid gardens, and kayaking under waterfalls. Kiana, Wally, and Pam gave me a rich taste of Hilo, Hawaii, that only a family living experience could provide. Aloha and Mahalo!

## REFLECTION

No matter what socio-economic background your students come from, their family members are valuable and have something to contribute. We must not assume that because the families are poor and living in the ghetto that they do not have riches to share. Because I honored each and every parent as an important dignitary, my class and I were gifted with many treasures.

As you think about the material in this chapter, ask yourself the following questions:

- Do I have any preconceived notions about my students or their families that I need to look at? What are they?

- What can I do to encourage more parental involvement?

- How can our families become resources that will benefit all of our students?

- How can my students and I learn more about the residents of our community and more effectively engage in community activities?

Kindergarten thespians dress in African clothing for our play,
"It Takes a Village."

## CHAPTER FIVE

# We're Off to See the Bad People

*"The seeds of transformation I plant will yield
a bountiful harvest."*

The excitement in Tamara's voice was palpable. "Linda, have you heard of this private school? It's a well-kept secret." Tamara went on and on about the school's curriculum and fabulous campus. I had not heard of the school she mentioned, in a small town near Denver. The school was making a concerted effort to reach out and offer scholarships to minority students and to create a more diverse mixture of faculty and families. Tamara had already registered her son Michael for the coming fall. She had also taken the liberty of telling the headmistress all about me. Tamara requested my résumé and copies of various newspaper articles about my teaching and gave them to the headmistress. The school needed a strong teacher in order to establish a kindergarten program. Up to this time, there had never been a kindergarten class, nor had there ever been an African-American teacher in the school's long and prestigious history.

After several days of listening to Tamara's effusive praise of the school, I decided to drive up and check it out for myself. I invited my friend Ruth to join me. When we drove onto the sprawling campus, we were impressed with the spectacular view. The school looked more like a small college. We found our way to the building that housed the office of the elementary school headmistress. The secretary showed us the way into her office. Ruth and I introduced ourselves and apologized for barging in unannounced. As the headmistress stood to greet us, I noticed that my résumé and the newspaper articles Tamara had provided were on her desk. "Why, Linda, what a pleasant surprise. We were just discussing your outstanding credentials."

After a brief chat, Ruth and I took our leave and headed back to Denver. Just as we approached the end of the exit lane off the highway, my car ran out of gas. Thank goodness we were right across the street from a service station. Ruth and I managed to push the car off to the side of the street. Was this an omen, a foreshadowing of what was to come when I became a teacher at that school? Or was it just a lesson that I should put gas in my car before the gauge gets to "E" and the orange gas pump light symbol has been on for a whole day?

I decided to accept the position. The administration made me an offer that was hard to resist. I had an apartment on a pristine campus with my classroom just a few steps up the hill from my deck. Through my windows I could see beautiful lakes, mountains, and Black Angus cattle, and I could watch the sunrise from my bed in the morning before I crawled out of it. I watched that same sun set in red, pink, orange, and purple splendor in the big sky at night. The delicious organic food at the school was prepared by a master chef. Lunch was like dining in a five-star restaurant. There was grilled fish, beef, chicken, seafood, salads, home-made soups, sandwich bars, grilled fresh vegetables, and breads and desserts baked daily. I had a brand new classroom twice the size of what I was used to, 16 students, and a full-time assistant in the classroom with me for the full eight-hour days. Heaven on earth! But this plot was sure to thicken.

Before teaching at this school, I had always chosen to teach in urban school settings. There was a greater need, I believed, for my teaching skills to educate poor children of color. It was not long after the school year started that I began to realize that I could make a powerful contribution by teaching these children as well. It was high time these privileged white children had the opportunity to learn about a culture different from their own. I was that opportunity, up close and personal, as their kindergarten teacher.

Since the elementary school was a new building, I was able to order the materials and furniture I wanted during the summer months. The classroom was organized and attractive from day one. The space was huge. In the reading corner, I placed a small aquarium filled with tropical fish, bookshelves, and an upholstered, child-size recliner under a massive, live ficus tree. Most of the wall beside the reading library was lined with windows that provided a view of the mountains. It was a quiet, sequestered nook. The parents and children always enjoyed sitting in that little recliner under the ficus tree and looking out at the pastoral view. No one ever wanted to leave that peaceful space.

At the other end of that same wall of windows was another reading area that would accommodate four students. It had miniature white wicker furniture, a matching table, and a rainbow of leveled book tubs. I always establish rituals, routines, and guidelines from the outset. For example, when I introduced the reading areas, I taught the children how many students could be in each area at one time. This way I avoided having to tell them that there are too many students in one area and asking some to leave. I determine the best management strategy through deep thought and envisioning. I visualize the children in the space. I think about how many books should be available and how many children could talk quietly without disturbing others in the room. Usually, the students don't challenge the number of students in an area or other rules of this nature. But there will always be at least one who will. When the challenge arises, I simply explain, "That is my rule." Nevertheless, I am flexible, and I constantly tweak the rules and learning environment to get the optimal learning result for each student. I keep focused on my objective: Each and every child must be safe and happy in order to learn, learn, learn.

The rest of the classroom was equally beautiful. There were many handsome, wooden-shelf units filled with Montessori materials, art pieces, live plants, fresh and dried flowers.

The school year got off to a great start. The parents were excited and very pleased with how their children were learning. That is, until January. In January, I taught the children about Dr. Martin Luther King, Jr. I kept the lessons as light as possible and appropriate for kindergarten-level children. Mostly, I told them stories rather than reading long books. I told them the story of how Yolanda, Dr. King's daughter, wanted to go to Fun Town, an amusement park in Atlanta and how Dr. King was very sad to have to tell his daughter that he could not take her to Fun Town because only white people could go there. I explained that people had made laws—not good laws—that said that black people could not go to Fun Town. But Dr. King told Yolanda that he was working very hard to change those bad laws to good laws so everyone, including black people, could go to Fun Town. Yolanda was much more understanding of why her father had to travel long distances and be away from his family after his explanation. She knew that her father, Dr. Martin Luther King, Jr., was working to change the laws so that she could go to Fun Town.

I also told them the story about the time when young Yolanda (now sadly deceased) took a candy bar from an airport gift shop without paying for it. When Yolanda took out her candy bar and, with ravenous gusto, took a huge bite, Dr. King stopped her and asked where she had gotten the candy bar. Yolanda admitted to her father that she had taken it from the gift shop. Dr. King asked her if she had paid for it. She said, "No, I just took it." Dr. King explained to his daughter that it is wrong to take things that do not belong to you. He told her that was stealing. Dr. King asked Yolanda to  wrap up the remainder of the candy bar and not to eat it. When he and Yolanda came back through the airport on their return flight, they made a stop at the gift shop, where Yolanda returned the candy bar and also paid for it.

By choosing powerful, child-centered stories like these, my aim was to give the children a visceral sense of who Dr. Martin Luther King, Jr., was as father, husband, human being, and civil rights leader. But one day, a problem arose when a parent came into my classroom and happened to see one page of a big book on Dr. King's life, which showed the Ku Klux Klan in white hoods and robes during a cross-burning ceremony, and she was alarmed. I had used the book only to show other pictures of Dr. King with his family. The book also contained great photographs of Rosa

Parks on the bus and of Dr. King with President Lyndon B. Johnson as he signed the Civil Rights Act of 1964. What the parent didn't know was that I hadn't shown the picture of the Ku Klux Klan to the children, but, sadly, she did not bother to ask me if I had before she alerted other kindergarten parents. She became the parents' spokesperson and marched off to see the headmistress. The picture in the book in my classroom soon became the buzz of the elementary school.

It is fascinating to me how we as human beings create drama when there is none. I can certainly be a drama queen on a dime. Lights, camera, action, let's rock! The mother's misunderstanding about the King biography became high drama for this small community. When I met with the mother and the headmistress, the mother reported that her son was very frightened that the Ku Klux Klan would break into their home and get him. I said, "Oh, just allay his fears. Explain to him that he does not have to worry about the Ku Klux Klan coming to get him. They might come to my house to get me, but not him." At the time, I thought my quip was quite amusing, but no one laughed at the joke but me.

We continued to talk for about half an hour more. I believe that the power to move mountains and change the world lives in communication—not just talking, mind you—but authentic communication, where people understand each other on a level beyond words. It is the whispering of hearts. That's what happened that day. Our hearts spoke and we were different when we came out of the headmistress' office. And despite my flippant remark, the fire of this drama had been extinguished.

The month of February arrived. Again, I reflected on the fact that I was the only African-American teacher ever to teach at this school. Who knows, I thought, I might be the last African-American teacher the children would ever have. I felt it incumbent upon me to teach them some African-American history, my history. Then I thought, "It is not African-

American history. It is not just my history. It is American History." This is not to say that someone other than an African American is incapable of teaching children about the experiences of African people enslaved and brought to the Americas. My concern was whether they would make an effort to teach the history.

It grieves me now to hear the argument that we should get rid of Black History Month. It is easy for people, usually not teachers, to sit around and pontificate about why it should just be American History. The fact remains that Black people's experiences and contributions to the building of this nation were not written in most history books or taught in schools. So, while it is American History, a conscious effort must be made to include Black History. Even with Black History Month, I see no visible trace of much of it being taught in schools these days. Back in the day, you could walk down the halls of a school during February and see students' research about famous Black Americans. Students had some sense of the Black American's presence in American History. Today, African Americans have become invisible in many school curricula. As Dick Gregory used to say, it is better to have the "shortest month of the year" to learn Black history and have it taught in schools than to have nothing at all.

Like the Martin Luther King, Jr., lessons, I made the stories appropriate for kindergarten children. I did not teach about famous Black American people. My lessons were about children in West Africa, the ancestral home of Black Americans. I decided we would present a play called "It Takes a Village." The play, which I adapted from the children's book of the same title by Jane Cowen Fletcher, is about a young girl who is left in charge of her little brother on market day in the village, while her mother sells mangos. The young girl is very proud to be grown up enough to take care of her little brother all by herself, but very soon the girl's brother gets lost. The little girl is relieved to discover that all the vendors have taken care of him. From this experience the girl's mother teaches her that West African children are not raised by the family alone. It takes a village to raise a child.

After I read the book to the children, I explained that we would be doing a play based on it, and they would wear African clothing for costumes. I collect African fabric remnants and was planning on using my stash for the play. One little boy, Harrison, looked very worried when I mentioned the African clothing. I asked him what was wrong. He said, "Well, we could wear the African clothes, but we will have to wear them on top of our uniform clothes 'cause, 'cause, 'cause African clothes are dirty and smelly and they have diseases in them and if they touch our skins we will get a rash."

There was such an innocence and purity in his voice. There was also a sincere willingness to please his teacher and go along with the plans even at the risk, he thought, of getting a disease. I took his little hands, plump and rounded with baby fat, in mine and looked into his eyes through my tears. I blinked my eyes quickly and tried to redistribute the tears to keep them from spilling over and running down my face. My attempt failed. I told Harrison and the 15 other children that they would not have to wear the dirty clothing of the children they had seen on television. I explained that not all children on the entire continent of Africa were sick and starving, but that too many were. It was now clear to me that we would have to go and buy new African fabric from a store, so they could see that it was clean and new. But this was going to require capital.

I wrote a grant application and sent it to the Teaching Tolerance branch of the Southern Poverty Law Center. I asked for $2,000. Half of it would be spent on the African fabric. The other $1,000 would be used to buy multicultural books for the new school library. At first I wondered how I would be able to justify asking for money for a school whose families owned two-million-dollar vacation homes in Aspen and whose children went to Venice for spring break. How would I write a grant for children and families who drove up in fancy cars and had individual nannies for each child in the family? Then it came to me. I began my grant with a quote often attributed to Edmund Burke: "All that is necessary for evil to triumph is that good men do nothing." I thought that it framed my argument quite well.

Despite the administration's efforts to make their campus more diverse, they were still in need of more cultural understanding and exposure. In the grant, I emphasized that the people at this elite institution are the very ones whose cultural competence should be raised. Girded with a broader understanding of different races, cultures, ethnicities, neighborhoods, and ways of being, these were the people with the money and power to make a huge difference in the world. We were awarded the grant for $2,000.

When the annual Scholastic blowout book sale came around, I had $1,000 in the bank—more than enough for a book-buying shopping spree. The sale was in a mammoth warehouse in an industrial area. I love buying books more than clothes or shoes, and that warehouse was crowded with books as far as my eyes could see. Books about many different cultures, families, faiths, and lifestyles filled the back seat of my car and trunk that afternoon. As I drove off, the rear of my 13-year-old Toyota Camry was almost dragging on the ground.

On the morning of our field trip to the African Boutique in Denver, the sun was shining, the temperature was moderate, and there was no snow on the highways. The mood of the children was mixed with joy and excitement, anticipation, and adventure. We were preparing to go out to board the bus when I noticed Harrison whispering to a group of boys and girls. I could tell something was amiss. One thing I will say for Harrison—that boy was a born leader. He was the one who would speak his truth and shake things loose. He had those six children sitting at his feet while he lectured them in muted tones so that I could not hear. They were all under the ficus tree in the corner with the panoramic view of the mountains, lakes, and the Black Angus cattle. He had one hand in his pocket. I imagined Socrates, Plato, or Aristotle would have looked this way while engaging his thinkers in deep dialectics.

When I walked over to the group, Gregory said, "Harrison said his mom called the police last night and that you are taking us to see the bad people." I took a deep, cleansing breath and looked toward those hills that I hoped would give me strength. I was thinking to myself, "How much more of this can I take?" I stayed calm and asked Gregory what he meant. The abridged version of Harrison's story was that his parents were so terrified that I was taking the class into a predominately African-American neighborhood in Denver that they called the police precinct the night before, requesting a full report of crime statistics in the area where the boutique was located. Harrison had overheard this conversation and some references to "bad people," and no doubt a few other adjectives and expletives. He was summarizing what he had overheard to the best of his ability. I thought, "Here we go again." I was not in a sympathetic, nurturing mood that morning. Harrison was on my last nerve, even though I knew that none of this was his fault. I just said in an irritated tone, "The people in Denver are not bad. They are just fine. Now, get on the bus."

The most gorgeous and interesting African boutique in Denver opened at 10 a.m. The owner, Ron, had agreed to meet my class at the boutique an hour earlier and give us an educational tour. When we walked in, there were so many beautiful, colorful treasures that it was almost sensory overload. The smell of pure incense and essential oils labeled "Nubian Heritage" and "The Real Deal" wafted through the room. The walls, and much of the floor space, were covered with African instruments, jewelry, dolls, baskets, and ceramics. There were precious artifacts of every texture, size, and color. Ron, a tall, handsome man in his mid-40s with more than a modicum of charm, was kind and knowledgeable, with a patient and child-friendly manner. Ron let the children examine anything they wanted to see up close. He opened essential oils for them to smell. We rubbed exotic lotions into our hands. We strung patterns of multicolored beads on top of the glass display cases. When Ron put on a CD of African music, that is when the celebration really began. All the children danced and whirled without inhibition, laughing loud and making fun of each other's movements.

Ron lowered the music and said, "So, I understand that you guys are here to get some African fabric, is that right?" All the children cheered. Ron led us upstairs to the second floor fabric room. The walls on the stairway were lined with carved wooden African masks. Each had a different expression. As I passed each one, I gave them a look that I hoped would silently communicate to them, "Y'all just don't know how deep all of this is."

At the top of the stairs was a room filled with nothing but African fabric. Instead of more loud cheering, the children became very quiet. They looked as though they were suddenly moving in slow motion, suspended in time and space. Their eyes were big as they slowly turned around and around, taking it all in. Ron taught us about the cloth and its geographical origins. There were mudcloth, batiks, laces, and prints woven with gold and silver threads. The children were moved, almost overwhelmed by such vibrant color and design. Ron explained to them that now they had to choose the fabric they liked best. This was a daunting task. After a while of deliberating over their choices, each child made a final selection. Ron cut a yard of fabric for each child, off bolts that stood almost as tall as the children. We descended the stairs, passing the masks with those same amused expressions. I gave the faces one last nonverbal communiqué as I walked down. This time it was, "It's all good in this neighborhood."

Ron offered to put each child's yard of fabric in a bag, but the children were so enamored with the cloth that they did not want the bag to cover its exquisite beauty. Everyone refused the bag. The children remained in this quiet, trancelike state during the bus ride back to school, sitting straight-backed and hugging the fabric close to their chests. I sat next to Zane, who was gazing out the window, as if he were reflecting on the experience he had that morning. Finally, he turned his gaze to me and said, "You are the only one who taught me that Dr. Martin Luther King was a 'civilized leader.'"

When we arrived back at the classroom, I was greeted by a few pink while-you-were-out messages on my desk. The parents wanted to know that their children had arrived back at school safely. After all, this had been a dangerous and risky trip! I called the parents right away to reassure them that their children were safe and the trip was a success.

The visit to the African boutique and the children's delight in the beautiful fabric each of them chose served to fuel their enthusiasm for the play we would produce. Because I have visited the West African country of Ghana twice and have amassed an interesting collection of artifacts to share with my students, I chose to focus on Ghana as the unit of study for the play. As we prepared for the production, we used a KWL chart on a large piece of chart paper to tap their existing knowledge of the country. In the first column I wrote with black marker what the children said they "know about Ghana." In the middle column we would list what they wanted to know, and in the last column what they had learned.

I have found the KWL chart to be a bit tricky as a tool to teach kindergartners. Kindergartners' confidence in their own wisdom and knowledge is something to be admired, but closely monitored. When I asked the children what they already "knew" about Ghana, the list was long: It is hot there. Lots of snakes are crawling around in Ghana. People don't wear any shoes in Ghana. The children don't have a house. Tatiana said she had visited Ghana many times and had seen some tigers. These were the "facts" they told me they knew. I did not correct them at that time. I just said, "Hmm, interesting," and did not write down anything they dictated in the "Know" column.

When we came to the "Want to Know" column, the exercise became more productive. In green marker, I wrote: Is Ghana near the Sistine Chapel? Do the children go to school with no clothes on? Do the children in Ghana like to eat pizza? Do their moms take them to the store to get toys? Do Santa's reindeer know how to fly to Ghana? If they are starving and don't have any food, why don't their moms take them to McDonald's and buy them a Happy Meal?

At the end of the unit of study, we completed the "Learned" column. I wrote in this column using purple marker so the children could see the contrast among the columns. The children had learned the names of the seven continents: North America, South America, Asia, Africa, Europe, Australia, and Antarctica. They could locate Ghana on a globe. They learned that some children go to school and wear uniforms and that they eat rice, peanut butter, chicken, bananas, okra, cassava, mangos, papaya, and sometimes a sweet, such as sesame candy or ice cream. Children go to church. Some children live in houses. They play on the beach. Some children in the village have a loom for weaving kente cloth on their front porch, with the father responsible for the weaving. The capital city of Ghana is Accra. African fabric is clean, beautiful, and disease-free and can be purchased here in the United States of America.

The KWL chart helped the children to understand what they thought they knew and what they had learned. They felt very proud and knowledgeable. When they tried to pin me down on whether Santa's reindeer knew how to find Ghana, I suggested that those who believed in Santa could write a letter to him and ask him this question, and I assured them that I would turn the letters over to the headmistress and ask her to mail them. This suggestion inspired some of the children to write letters to Santa. Tatiana, a slight girl with freckles and red-orange hair, would not write a letter. She said that it was silly and that the others could write all they wanted to, but Christmas was over.

The play was a great success. I incorporated the reading, geography, and social studies lessons into the script for the production. The children learned voice projection, speaking and listening skills, concentration, and stage etiquette. But the most exciting, or as one child wrote, the most "eggsiding" part was the costumes. I hired a seamstress to make some two-piece skirts and tops for the girls and dashikis and kufis for the boys. Some fabric was left uncut and I used it to wrap the children. I knew I would be using the untailored cloth in the years to come; I would be able to wrap children regardless of their size. On the day of the play, the children wore the African fabric with honor and appreciation. Their parents and friends filed into the large meeting room not knowing what to expect, but they could not hide their joy when they saw their children enter the room wearing that beautiful clothing. There were no curtains to open, so the children walked in single file and took their places on the small stage. Some carried African baskets containing plastic fruit, peanuts in the shells, and folded fabric on their heads. Some children portrayed vendors selling livestock, peanuts, water, and mats. We had practiced the blocking, so they knew where to stand. Bethany announced, "The cast will be available to sign autographs immediately following the performance."

The children enjoyed delivering their lines in strong voices out toward their families. At the end of the performance, I presented each child with a bouquet of three fresh carnations tied together with a huge green ribbon. And, indeed, the little kindergarten thespians signed autographs. When we started rehearsing the play, the penmanship of most of the children was excellent, but they wrote slowly and with great deliberation. So I taught them about signatures and explained how a signature could help them write faster, thereby enabling them to sign more autographs for their adoring fans. During a writer's workshop just before the performance, I had taught the children to make the first capital letter of their names and then end the signature with whatever kind of squiggly configuration they liked. They got a big kick out of writing their signatures, especially when the upper-grade students, whom I had asked to play the part of adoring fans, waited patiently in queue.

I wish I could say that congratulations flowed copiously from the parents, and that negative attitudes about race, religion, nationality, or geographical location were transformed forever for the good. This did not happen.

The overall response to the production from administration and families was that of quiet acceptance. The audience smiled often and applauded vigorously for the children's performance.

But little shifts in the attitudes of the children and parents were noticeable. In their own subtle ways, they appreciated the new experiences. The children began to respond to the few African-American children at the school differently. One girl in my class asked an

African-American girl if she lived in Africa. Curiosity had been sparked. A dialogue had begun. Braden's mom volunteered to come to the school library and paste labels in the new multicultural books. The labels were an acknowledgement of thanks to the Teaching Tolerance branch of the Southern Poverty Law Center who had given me the grant to buy the books.

The day after the play, Emma said she liked Africa and Ghana and asked if we could go to Ghana on the bus tomorrow. I smiled as I visualized Harrison's mom calling Ghana to get a report on the recent crime statistics in Accra.

## REFLECTION

When I started the year teaching at this school, the children and I planted tulip bulbs. In spring, the tulips burst forth in a glorious array of vibrant colors, like those in our African cloth. As teachers, we sow seeds of knowledge, hope, love, and cultural understanding. We trust that these seeds will be nurtured in the warmth of the rich, dark earth of the minds we impact. We continue to teach each day, believing that we have planted well and that there will be a bountiful harvest in due season. But many times we do not see our harvest. Sometimes we have gone on to plant in another land. Yet our joy comes from knowing that we have given our personal best to enlighten minds, to lift spirits, to transform the world one child and family at a time.

As you think about the material in this chapter, ask yourself the following questions:

How have you handled situations in which children have repeated negative messages that they've heard at home to their classmates?

Do your students experience a diversity of cultures in their everyday lives? In what ways have you provided them with authentic cross-cultural experiences? Do you feel you had enough preparation and follow-up for these events?

How do you address students' perceptions of "good" and "bad" people?

Have you ever had a parent or administrator take issue with the content or approach of one of your lessons? What did you do in that situation?

Who says a mousetrap has to be a little, flat rectangle?

## CHAPTER SIX

# Mice in the Classroom,
# Men in Space

*"Creativity surrounds and infuses me and
I honor it in others."*

ॐ

Webster defines a phobia as "a persistent, irrational fear of a specific object, activity or situation." You could say, given this definition, that I have a phobia about mice. Yes, I know they are little and I am big and they are afraid of me. It does not matter. If I see a mouse, my behavior is irrational at best. Don't get me wrong, or as the kids say, "don't get it twisted." Custodians in school buildings do a fantastic job of keeping the buildings clean and functioning properly. But despite their diligent efforts, mice can still find their way into classrooms.

It was January, the beginning of a new year and the second semester of kindergarten. I had gotten some rest during the holiday break and was eager to see my students' smiling, happy faces. I knew they would all want to talk to me at once and tell me everything that had happened while we were out of school.

The clock on the wall above the door of my classroom read 7:10 a.m. I turned on the lights and put my things down on my desk at the back of the room. It was great to be back at school. With my peripheral vision, I caught a glimpse of a shadow moving quickly by the baseboards under the shelves to my right. I knew that I had seen something, but I could not admit it to myself. I chose that ancient river in Egypt, "De Nile," and I stayed at my desk organizing my lesson plans. "You did not see anything," was my internal mantra. I successfully put the moving shadow out of my mind and went over to dust and straighten the shelves. I kept paper, pencils, and markers available near the manipulative materials on the shelves so the children could write and illustrate their work. A stack of primary writing paper had been cut into thick strips. The edges of the paper strips were jagged, as though they had been cut with pinking sheers. That Egyptian River is deep, I tell you, deep. And I was sinking down to its depths. I took the shredded papers off the shelves and threw them into the trash. As I walked across the room I noticed some kind of little black pellets on the floor. I was about to get the broom and sweep up the little somethings when the bell rang. It was time for the children to come in. Luckily, I spotted the custodian in the hallway, and I asked her to come in and clean the floor.

As I had anticipated, the children were so happy to see me and each other. Some were wearing new clothes they had gotten as Christmas presents. The girls were wearing bright pink and purple barrettes, velour jogging suits, and plastic jewels on both wrists. The boys showed off new jeans, shirts, and tennis shoes that lit up when they walked. Uriel gave me what he called a "Christmas" present, wrapped in the sale papers from our largest supermarket chain. I thanked him and gave him a big hug. "Should I open it now?" I asked, so honored that he had thought of me during the holidays. He shook his head up and down quickly. Under the paper, which told me the price of cranberries, ham, collard greens, and cilantro, was a brand new calendar complements of "Raymond's Service Station." I was very touched and gave Uriel another big hug to express my genuine gratitude. "Don't you start crying, stop it, stop it," I told myself.

We were well into our morning ritual of greetings, songs, the calendar, and the weather report when I saw two shapes zip behind the shelves. Kwame pointed and began jumping up and down. "Look Ms. Alston, that's two mouses over there." Children will shock you into knowing the truth whether you want to know it or not. They will call a mouse a mouse. There were no more pyramids, sphinxes, and sailing on feluccas for me that day. My trip to Egypt had ended. There were mice in my classroom!

Before that day, I had thought of myself as one of those "she-roic" teachers who would throw myself in the path of danger to protect the children. And I probably would, except these were mice. The wooden pointer with the apple on the end fell from my hand to the floor, and I ran out of the room like a screaming mimi, leaving all the children in the room. I was headed down the hall with no particular destination in mind, when suddenly, I made a U-turn and sprinted back to Mr. Herman's kindergarten classroom, directly across the hall from mine.

When he saw my face, he knew I was in distress. I could not speak. My left hand was over my mouth, and with my right hand I pointed to my classroom across the hall, which had erupted with laughter. All the while I was dancing around, and little squeaking noises were escaping my mouth through my cupped fingers. Mr. Herman said, "Got a little emergency, Linda? Go on, I'll watch your class for you." He thought I was dancing around because I had to go to the bathroom really badly. After all, there had been numerous occasions where this in fact was the case. I shook my head no and kept pointing toward my room. My students were at the door and out in the hall, still cracking up. Kwame said, "Mr. Herman, we got some mouses in our room, and Ms. Alston is scared." Mr. Herman joined in the children's laughter. Mr. Herman's kindergartners started laughing and ran to the door to try to see the mice. This situation was out of control.

At an urban area school, when you hear screaming, you don't take it lightly. Teachers down the hall heard the commotion and one of them called the principal, who in turn called the school's business manager and custodian. They all came running downstairs to the kindergarten classrooms with their walkie-talkies. As Prince would say, "Dig, if you will, the picture." Still in an irrational frame of mind, I left the children in my classroom with the business manager and informed the principal that I was going home and that the secretary could call a substitute teacher to replace me. Furthermore, I let her know that I would not be returning until the mice were gone.

The principal said that our school already had a contract with an exterminating service and they would take care of the problem. "Well, it is obvious that what this company is doing it is not working," I said, wondering who was going to go back into the room and get my purse, which held my getaway car keys. Recently I had read about a space shuttle having astronauts orbit out in space for months and they had come back safely to tell about it. After gulping down half a bottle of water, I told the principal, "If we have scientists who are smart enough to launch astronauts into outer space for months at a time, surely, we are smart enough to get rid of mice." In the end, I decided to stay at school in my classroom for the remainder of the day, but my assistant had arrived so I felt a little safer.

By the next morning, the custodian and her crew had cleaned the room and blocked an area where the mice could have been coming into the room. I was still a bundle of nerves but I tried not to think about the rodents, and I did most of my teaching right by the door. Mr. Herman waved at me and laughed every time he passed by and saw me. He knew I didn't normally stand there.

That afternoon, an interesting thing happened. A group of boys and girls were working quietly and with focused intention in the block area. After more than an hour, they invited me to see their construction, a huge and elaborate configuration of blocks that they explained was a mousetrap. After they had stopped laughing and had some time to reflect, the children felt compassionate and were motivated to find a solution to their teacher's problem. Kayla said, "Ms. Alston, you was scared of those mice so we built this trap to catch them so you don't have to be scared no more." The construction was amazing. The children had used every block in the center and added many other materials to their project. What impressed me most was how they explained the cause and effect of what would happen as each mouse ran through this maze. When a mouse would run through the maze and come out, the last block would fall on its head. These little architects had included the toy wooden stove from the dramatic play area as a prop. They had remembered that turning the little red knobs on the stove caused a squeaking sound and it was Ian's job to stand by the stove and turn the knob when it was time for a squeak. That is how detailed the work of the children had been in building this mousetrap.

The children built mousetraps every day for the entire week, and the traps became more and more elaborate. I wrote copious notes to document what the children had done and what they were learning. They were working together cooperatively, learning problem-solving and higher-order thinking skills. The mousetrap construction required planning, talking to each other, delegating tasks, balancing blocks, comparing sizes, geometry, and design skills. This was creativity at its finest. I did not impose myself upon the group while the children worked, but I lurked near the construction site to observe what they did and hear what they were saying. The children planned their own extensions of the project. They wrote stories and drew maps and pictures of the mousetrap. The children were the ones who organized, planned, and implemented the entire project, all without teachers.

Fundamentally, I believe that there are many different styles of teaching that address the different needs of children, and a teacher should find the style that best suits him or her. What has worked for me is an eclectic blend of best practices from many different approaches. My professional background in literacy, which is my passion, includes a master's degree in language, literacy, and culture and the teaching of the linguistically diverse. I also draw from Montessori training, Reggio Emilia workshops, Reading Recovery, Success For All, Learning Network, Balanced Literacy, and the Vygotskian approach to guide my teaching. I have chosen not to ascribe strictly to one way of teaching. I have a core belief that my first obligation is to help a child learn effectively and meet with success. Children learn differently. If a child is not making academic progress, I do not stop until I find methods that work for him. This is how I differentiate instruction and individualize my teaching.

It is extremely important to allow time for children to be creative and to think. The mousetrap project is an example of what happens when children are given a chance to solve a real problem and to take ownership of their own learning. Sometimes less is more. We don't always need an abundance of sophisticated props and materials. The children used the blocks and whatever else was available to them to build the mousetrap. They used their ability to pretend and imagine. I believe these are important tools, ones not to be excluded from the child's school experience from pre-K through graduate work. If the child chooses to study architecture later in life, she must still be able to imagine a great building or design. This creation occurs in her mind first before she puts the lines to paper and her creation is constructed.

The creativity of children is extraordinary. Another such example of their brilliance occurred in the dramatic play area of the classroom, which I had set up to be "The Justina Ford Pediatric Clinic." Our clinic was named for the first African-American woman doctor in the state of Colorado. It was part of an integrated unit of study that included reading, writing, and telling time, and drew from mathematics, science, social studies, communication, and play. We set up the patients' waiting room and created jobs for role playing. One job was that of the receptionist. This job description included welcoming the patient (a stuffed animal or doll) and its parent (the student who had brought the stuffed animal). The receptionist also answered the turquoise blue plastic princess phone, wrote messages, and set up appointments. Two doctors were on duty to see patients, and the job of doctor rotated every two days. That made a total of four children in the clinic, which I considered a good number. Parents and friends had donated real medical materials including gauze, Band-Aids, masks, stethoscopes, and two small white doctor's coats, which fit the kindergartners perfectly.

I wrote up an "intake questionnaire" that had to be filled out by the doctors on duty. The doctors read the questionnaire to the parent of the patient. They needed to know the name, age, and birth weight of the patient, his or her medical insurance carrier, and the symptoms he or she was experiencing. On the wall in the clinic was a sight word list of possible symptoms the parent of the patient could read in case she could not think of any. The list included the words *cough, fever, runny nose, sore throat,* and *stomach ache.* For the doctors the sight word choices were *cold, flu,* and *upset stomach*—all diagnoses the doctors might make as they examined their patients. The medical recommendations given by the doctors spurred us to create another list of sight-word phrases: *rest in bed, drink liquids,* and *take vitamin C.* I tried to choose words that I thought the children could relate to as kindergartners.

It didn't take long before the imaginations of the children far exceeded my expectations. When I reviewed what the doctors had recorded on the intake forms, I found diagnoses like "bran cansr" and "to mush smokn." Some of the patients whose mom or dad brought them to the clinic included a star-studded list of celebrities. There was Big Bird, Ernie, Burt, and Oscar from "Sesame Street," and Barbie and Ken of Malibu, California. They all left the clinic bandaged up beyond recognition and well on their way to a full recovery.

One day Stephanie was the receptionist. There were no patients in the waiting area. The doctors were busy straightening up all the materials on the tables covered with white sheets that had been donated by our local Holiday Inn. Stephanie filled in the down time with the use of her imagination. Suddenly, the turquoise princess phone rang but the sound was audible only to Stephanie. "Hello, hello, Justina Ford Medical Clinic, how may I assist you?" she greeted the caller with the mandatory smile in her voice. "Yes, who is this? Yes, okay, okay, okay, okay. Yes, I will tell Linda," which is what the children called me at that school. Stephanie said goodbye and hung up the phone. She began to write on the note pad that was on her receptionist desk.

After about half an hour Stephanie brought the paper to me. She reported that Hollywood had called and asked if I could star in a movie with Billy Dee Williams as my leading man. They had to start the shoot right away and asked if I could fly out immediately. I thanked Stephanie for the message and was understandably overwhelmed with excitement. I began to pace the floor with the back of my hand to my forehead. "Wow, I can't believe this amazing offer," I said to Stephanie, which was a little private joke on her. "I have some serious decisions to make. Oh, oh, I feel faint. I need to check myself into the clinic." I stumbled to the clinic and let the doctors perform triage. By this time, Clifford the Big Red Dog was in the waiting room with his dad, but he had to keep waiting. This was an emergency, and I needed immediate attention.

When I teach, I tell the children about myself and allow them to get to know me not just as their teacher but as a person. These kindergartners knew that I like fried chicken and Pink Lady apples and that I am always on a diet except when I am not. Stephanie even remembered how much I love the actor Billy Dee Williams. Without the down time that provided Stephanie with the opportunity to write the message, I might have missed out on this fun time shared with the children. It was also time well spent with Stephanie as she used her imagination and creativity to compose a story that involved writing, spelling, and speaking. Creativity and academic rigor are not mutually exclusive. They are as integrated and intricately woven together as the notes of a great symphony and every bit as harmonious.

## REFLECTION

Children are children, and I am a champion of their right to have the experience of childhood. While we must make sure they get a good education and solid foundation for the future, the beauty, magic, and wonder of childhood is right now. Children are creative and imaginative. We all have curricula that we must follow, but we can teach the required lessons and teach them well, while allowing children the opportunity to express their creative genius.

As you think about the material in this chapter, ask yourself the following questions:

- Have your students ever turned a challenging classroom situation into a learning opportunity? Explain.

- Do you build time into your day for children to express their natural curiosity and creativity? What are some ways you can make time for such open-ended explorations? How can you "justify" these detours to your administrators?

- Have you ever shared some of your own personal fears with your students? How did they respond? What are the advantages of sharing such vulnerabilities?

- How do you differentiate instruction in your classroom? In what situations do your students learn best? How can you tailor your instructional methods to make sure that all of your students succeed?

My students gather in the radiant glow of the "glass" bottle tree.

## CHAPTER SEVEN

# Creating the Glittery Glass Bottle Tree

*"I leave room for that which inspires me."*

✣

If you were on "Jeopardy" and Alex Trebek gave the answer, "What a teacher does to prepare for her students the following day," I doubt that your answer would be, "What is baking cornbread?" If you were my mother, Lucille, you would win the round. Mama taught elementary school in Louisiana for more than 30 years. Her first teaching positions were in small country churches. In the evening she would bake cornbread for her multigrade class. In the morning, she would pack up the cornbread and some dried beans and walk miles to the church school. Before the students arrived, Mama would put a pot of beans on the heater to simmer. By noon, lunch was ready to be served. The children knelt down on the floor and leaned on the wooden pews to write their lessons.

Before she passed away, Mama loved telling me those stories about her early days of teaching. When school districts started to implement new programs referred to as "site-based management," "multiage class-rooms" and "looping," Mama would fall out laughing and say, "Chile' they think that is new? I was managing everything, including cleaning, cooking, and teaching in the church. All the children were in the same class no matter what grade or age. And I 'looped' up with all of them every year. What do they think is new about all that?"

By the time she was ready to retire, the schools and teaching conditions had improved. She taught in a school building with indoor restrooms and other "luxuries" that Mama loved. To Mama, glitter was a treasure she reserved for special projects. Whenever she had to create a bulletin board for the school, Mama would beautify it with her prized glitter. I think that is why I love glitter so much today. My teacher friend Brooke says my motto in life should be, "When all else fails, sprinkle some glitter on it." And she's right, because when I found myself presented with the opportunity to use the largest quantity of glitter in my teaching career, I seized it.

From time to time, both teaching and life can feel repetitive and lackluster. Correction: life is never really without excitement and newness, but I sometimes start to experience it as though it were. That's around the time I take on a big project to get myself inspired. I know when I have found one of these projects because the idea lights me up. Suddenly, I feel enlivened and creative, with teaching ideas flooding my consciousness. This is what happened when I got the inspiration to create a unit of study on the "glass bottle tree." Oh, I should also add that these units of study are almost always written by me and they usually go beyond the prescribed curriculum. Packaged thematic units are great, but the ones that I create around an idea that genuinely hooks me are my best.

As a girl growing up in Louisiana, I remembered seeing trees in the front yards of rural homes festooned with colorful glass bottles. I never knew the significance of the glass bottle tree nor why they were there. After hearing about the art exhibit on a university campus in Denver of bottle tree sculptures designed by a local artist, I reflected on the glass bottle trees from my childhood as well as the one I saw in the movie *Ray*, which recounts the life of legendary singer Ray Charles, and in another one of my favorite films, *Because of Winn-Dixie*. This film pictures the glass bottle tree in the backyard of Gloria Dump, a character played by Cicely Tyson.

There are different cultural interpretations of the glass bottle tree. One story maintains that the glass bottle tree stands guard in front of the home to protect the family from negative energy. The negative energy is lured to the light that plays on the colorful bottles hanging from the tree. The wind blows through the bottles and creates sounds similar to those of a wind chime. Negative spirits come too close and become trapped inside the bottles. In a different story, the bottles contain good spirits of a family's ancestors. If any harm should approach the house, the benevolent spirits of the ancestors come out of the bottles and drive the evil away.

When we started the study of the glass bottle tree, I did not know that one of the legendary origins traced back to the Democratic Republic of the Congo on the African continent. The mother and grandparents of Terry, a kindergarten boy in our class, came from this part of the world.

Terry's mom and grandparents were able to contribute a wealth of knowledge to our study. They spoke fluent French, and Terry taught us to say phrases in one of the languages spoken in the Congo.

Several parents and some of my personal friends accompanied us on our trip to the bottle tree exhibit. The children enjoyed being on a university campus and asked very thoughtful and intelligent questions of the artist. It is good to expose our children to art galleries and beautiful experiences. Some hesitate to take the children to these places for fear they might break something precious. For weeks before we go on such an excursion, I teach my students how to behave in such an environment, and I explain that we do not touch anything unless someone invites us to do so. The children were so well behaved that the university professors were amazed and complimented them on their excellent behavior. When we returned to the classroom, I surprised the children with colorful bottles of juice that I had purchased from the supermarket. There's nothing I love more than extending a thematic unit.

I decided to make a glass bottle tree in our classroom. Each child would decorate his or her own glass bottle to hang on the tree. Now I had to figure out where I would get glass bottles. One night I was sitting in my bed at home trying to solve this problem. As I thought about different beverages that came in small glass bottles and how we could get people to start recycling them, I was drinking water from a plastic bottle. Then it hit me. I did not have to be so literal. Instead of glass bottles, we could use the plastic bottles that were readily available at school and at my house. The plastic bottles were lighter, and here was the best part: if we coated them with glue, we could adorn them with glitter.

In no time our class had more than enough plastic bottles for our project. I ordered big bottles of glitter in blue, red, green, yellow, orange, purple, silver, and gold. This glitter business was exciting. We hung our "glass" bottles from a tree branch that I salvaged from a pile of trimmings near the school and dragged into the classroom. Now, if that wasn't pretty enough, I brought in a string of Christmas tree lights and wove them around the glittered bottles. When the children came into the classroom in the morning, only the natural light from the windows filled the room. Our "glass" bottle tree was a sparkling triumph of stunning beauty and indescribable joy.

When asked what spirit they wanted to fill their bottles with, each child's answer was richer than the one before. Our bottles were filled with the spirits of happiness, healing and wholeness, fiscal responsibility, justice and racial harmony, domestic tranquility, morality, and loving sibling relationships.

Of course, the children did not have this vocabulary. I taught it to them. Our mantra was, "Big words don't frighten us." Socratic questioning—asking the children to fish around until they found the right answer (in this case, words that describe sophisticated concepts)—was sometimes not the most efficient teaching method for my students. After all, as Betty Hart and Todd Risley report in *Meaningful Differences in the Everyday Experience of Young American Children* (1995), by the age of three, my students (and kids like them) had heard nearly 8 million words *fewer* than their peers in professional families, which had caused a 300 spoken word deficit. I was not going to be stingy with vocabulary.

One of the skills I learned from teaching the Success For All program is to avoid teaching vocabulary by having children guess what a word means. For example, if the vocabulary word is "antlers," I should not ask five children what they think the word "antlers" means, especially not kindergartners. They will guess so many tangential answers that everybody ends up confused. The danger is that children often remember one of their classmates' guesses instead of the true definition. For this reason,

I taught my students the definition of antlers as "a solid, branched horn of the deer family," period! My students needed direct instruction. If they didn't receive a solid, world class, cutting edge education, it seemed as though their very lives were at stake. There was no time to lose. I gave the children all that I had and withheld nothing. I taught them how to express themselves through a lavish, full-bodied use of the English language. The children were empowered by the praise they received from adults when they could articulate their ideas with power.

One such example was a story shared by the parents of one of my students. Friends were visiting at their home one evening and Shanti, my student, and the visiting little girl were playing together. Shanti did something to make the visiting child angry. The girl said, "I'm not going to be your friend anymore." Shanti's response was, "But you have to be my friend because we are peaceful, loving, brilliant children." The visiting girl's parents overheard this comment coming from Shanti and said, "Where on earth is she learning all that from?" Shanti's mom's answer was, "Linda."

My students experienced harsh realities in their daily lives that mirror the troubling nature of our society. When I drew them out by asking questions or brainstorming, there was often a barrage of undesirable answers. So, when I asked what each one wanted to put into their bottle as a good spirit, the children got lost in a negative recall of their environments. It is not enough for me to just follow the teacher's manual and ask the children to "activate their scheme," meaning to think about what they already know about a subject in their personal experience. I don't leave them hanging. I never let them fail. In the students' precious little attempts to describe something good, the bad things that haunted them came forth. I immediately taught them a way to express positively what would be present if the bad thing was gone.

| *Child's Answer* | *New Vocabulary and Expression* |
| --- | --- |
| "My daddy don't be hurtin' my mom" | "HEALING AND WHOLENESS" |
| "People don't have to rob no banks" | "FISCAL RESPONSIBILITY AND HONESTY" |
| "The cops won't pull you over 'cause you Mexican" | "JUSTICE AND RACIAL EQUALITY" |
| "My uncle won't beat his girlfriend at the cook-out" | "DOMESTIC TRANQUILITY" |
| "Nobody don't be watchin' no dirty movies" | "CLEAN, MENTAL MORALITY" |
| "My sister will stop hitting me" | "LOVING SIBLING RELATIONSHIPS" |
| "Nobody take kids out their house and kidnap them" | "SAFETY AND SECURITY FOR ALL CHILDREN EVERYWHERE" |
| "Don't break in nobody's house and break into their van" | "RESPECT FOR THE RIGHTS AND PROPERTY OF OTHERS" |
| "People don't be drivin' drunk" | "SOBRIETY" |

In the right column were the good spirits who lived in our bottles. The left column unveiled the fears that weighed heavily on the minds of these little 5-year-old children and exposed these demons to the light. Perhaps I provided the only safe space they had to express their fears and replace them with the possibility of goodness and hope for a better way and a better day. The children took a stand for the good spirit that lived in their glittered bottle, not just for themselves. In other words, they embraced the possibility that their good spirit was a force for good in the world. For example, Nelson Mandela took a "stand" for justice in South Africa. As long as he remained in jail and did not give up on believing that apartheid could end, the possibility lived because one man stood for it. Mother Teresa took a stand for healing (ending poverty and hunger). Her spirit embodies that conviction and possibility.

Each child held in his or her consciousness the possibility of what the good spirit in their bottle represented. Each child gained a more positive outlook on life because each one believed that what the spirit in their bottle stood for was possible not only for their community, but for the planet. As we replaced the bad concerns with the new language and expression of the thought, the room filled with joy and lightness. The children inspired me so intensely with the wordsmithing and the presence of their positive spirits that I ran a lap around the classroom in celebration of each new paradigm they declared. They all laughed at me and cheered each other.

There would be no space on my teacher evaluation form or end-of-the-year test results sheet to document the wondrous catharsis for the children the glass bottle tree unit of study had caused. But these are the memories of kindergarten my students cherish and share with me when they return to visit 25 years later. When I went to Robert's house for his teacher home visit, it made me smile to see his glitter bottle hanging in the tree out front. It was a shiny, cobalt blue. After saying hello and welcoming me into his home, the whole family asked if I had seen Robert's bottle outside in the tree. There was no way it could be missed. It was my hope that the dazzle and goodness of the glittery, glass bottle tree would illumine the children's lives forever.

## REFLECTION

I love teaching because I continue to learn. When I am inspired and enthusiastic about what we are learning, it is infectious. The children catch my enthusiasm and they become excited also. I remain open to all there is around me that makes me curious and passionate about learning. I share this knowledge with my students, and they respond to the joy and vitality. They love a good party. My thematic units and special projects spark interest and freshness. During the glass bottle tree unit, the children wrote more stories, calculated more mathematics, asked more questions, and shared more with their parents because of the excitement of the glass bottle tree project. They had something to talk about at the end of the day beyond the routine studies. When children love learning and are excited and interested in what they are studying, they will make greater academic progress. As I follow district curricula and fulfill the state standards, I find time for expansion and enrichment, even when it means extra time, resources, and work.

As you think about the material in this chapter, ask yourself the following questions:

- ❦ What kinds of classroom projects inspire you? Describe a unit of study that you created for your students that resulted from your own inspiration. How did your enthusiasm affect your students?

- ❦ If you write your own units of study, how can you make sure that you are still meeting your content standards?

- ❦ What are some ways to involve students' families in your classroom projects? What are the advantages of such participation?

- ❦ What are your feelings about introducing sophisticated words and concepts to your students? How can you make sure that students fully understand such words?

My classroom is the children's ship and they take the helm with intention and élan.

CHAPTER EIGHT

# I'll Never Teach Another Day . . . Until Tomorrow

*"I rise up, draw in the life breath and march on
'til victory is won."*

The snow-crowned mountains, indigo lakes, picturesque sky, and golden aspen trees in Colorado are as beautiful as the pictures. That's what I found out when I moved to Denver in 1987. I had thought that the pictures I saw on posters and calendars were aesthetically enhanced. People would laugh at me when I said repeatedly, "It's just like the calendars." It seemed to me that moving from Milwaukee, Wisconsin, to a new city and state would be a perfect time to also get the heck out of Dodge—and my Dodge was teaching. When I first settled into my new home, I accepted a job as a fashion consultant. I liked the experience of working in a business owned by a woman and I dreamed of owning my own business. Instead of getting into another fashion salon, I decided to open an exercise business.

"No Sweat Body Toning" was the name of my new salon. It was a clean, classy business in a strip mall with seven motorized toning tables, massage room, and make-up and accessories area. It was another one of my side ventures away from teaching. Other detours off the teaching path had been beauty consultant, fashion boutique manager, interior decorator, and sales representative for encyclopedias, long distance phone services, and exotic fruit juices. Yes, I have tried to escape teaching many times, believe that. Left to my own designs, I might have chosen a profession that was more lucrative and glamorous, like acting or being a singer like Nancy Wilson or Nina Simone, except for one little challenge . . . I can't sing.

But there was no escaping my divine calling. Teaching had me. One day while in my toning salon, minding my own business, I started talking about Montessori education to Sharon, one of my clients, and how perfect it would be for her two children. I got myself so worked up and excited about education that she and I decided to drive to a school so she could actually see what I was describing.

I left my manager, Carol, tending the store, and off Sharon and I went to the school. My dear friend Paula was the principal. Sharon and I were sitting in her office casually discussing the school when Paula told me that plans were being made to start a Montessori program in a child development center two blocks down the street. She said I really should speak with the executive director, Anna Jo Haynes, about her vision for the school. I went to speak with Anna Jo dressed for success, in a pink and white sweat suit, tennis shoes, and a scarf tied on my head. The next morning I had a full-time job as the director of the center and a dilemma on my hands: How would I spin both plates—my business and this new position?

I arranged for Carol to work longer hours at the salon. Carol took over "No Sweat Body Toning," and I threw myself full-tilt boogie into working at the Mile High Northeast Child Development Center. Recently, it has been renamed "Northeast Montessori Early Learning Center," joining 11 other early learning centers that eventually adopted the Montessori model.

Enrollment was low at the center. The classrooms were drab and depressing, and the children were destroying the place toy by plastic toy. When I am preparing a new learning environment, it takes time and thought. Dorothy, the dietitian in the building, would often find me standing in the center of the room staring into the cosmos. She would interrupt my reverie with a snack because I had forgotten to eat. I was too busy planning the space for the children. I asked myself questions like: Is there enough light here for the writing center? What will be the traffic flow through this area? How will the children's work in content areas like mathematics, literacy, sensory materials, art, and science be arranged on the shelves? The dull, uninspiring rooms soon became exciting, colorful, and engaging,

In order to gather materials I needed to organize the classroom, I started visiting Goodwill, Arch, and Salvation Army stores. I purchased wicker baskets, trays, flower vases, and beautiful antiques. I would be driving down a street and it seemed as though my car took on a mind of its own and would swerve and turn into one of these stores.

There were programs for various addictions like alcohol, drugs, food, and gambling, but I was not aware of any for secondhand store shopping. I thought at times that I might have to start a program called Thrift Store Shoppers Anonymous.

At first, José and Cierra were the only two students in the center. Cierra liked to play at the water table all day. José liked to cuss, break things, and punch Cierra every chance he got. I found a journal in which the former director had been documenting José's behavior. There was enough incriminating evidence in that notebook to send José up the river for life, even at only 5 years old. I worked one-on-one with each child, giving them lessons with the learning materials to help them learn to work independently. For example, I taught Cierra how to complete a hundred board grid by placing tiles in order from one to one hundred. I taught José the sounds and names of the letters of the alphabet by having him shape them in play dough or trace them on sandpaper and in powdered Kool-Aid. After the children were able to center themselves and feel more grounded, I taught them to work together. Cierra and José learned how to take turns and respect each other. They became friends. Cierra stopped hurling water toys at José, and José no longer viewed Cierra as his personal punching bag.

Word got out that things were changing at the center, and our enrollment grew. But with the influx of the new students came new problems. The number of students grew to about 20, but I wished for the days when there was only Cierra, José, and me. The new students had some serious behavior issues. They would spit all over the materials. They ran through the rooms and would not settle down for a group time and they left the rooms in shambles. Mealtimes meant food fights. I thought about my exercise salon and how peaceful and beautiful it was with adults and adult conversation. What had I gotten myself into AGAIN? This new teaching challenge was wearing me out. I called my friend Paula and complained and cried. Every day I would quit, but the way I knew that I hadn't really quit is that I would notice myself there the next morning at six. When I want to remind myself what commitment means, I think back on this experience. It does not matter how you feel, what you think, or how many tantrums you have. Commitment means being true to your word. The power of my commitment would bring me back. And each day that I came back, the children learned and their behavior improved.

One day Anna Jo came for a visit and brought with her some unexpected guests: Colorado Governor Roy Romer and his wife, Mrs. Bea Romer, along with the superintendent of Denver public schools and other friends of quality early childhood education. When they entered the first classroom, José ran up to Anna Jo to show her his work. My assistant and I held our breaths. We didn't know what José would say. Was he going to cuss out Anna Jo and the governor and his wife? We let out a sigh of relief when José enthusiastically explained that he had finished his map of the world and was starting another major work project. Anna Jo smiled and complimented José on his success. She showed the visitors the journal of José's behavior from just a few weeks ago. They could not believe this was the same child, and actually she could not believe it either.

José's classmates were working away at a wide assortment of activities. Some were doing math, reading books, and washing china dishes. Others were washing tables, folding cloth napkins, and transferring beads from the left ceramic bowl to the right to learn concentration and directionality for reading. Cierra was painting a picture that would later hang on the wall in the classroom art gallery alongside prints of Van Gogh's *Sunflowers*, Monet's *Water Lilies*, Henry O. Tanner's *The Banjo Lesson*, and James Chapin's *Ruby Green Singing*.

The children had progressed into an academic work rhythm. They were self-regulating, and life was good. I was quitting less frequently now, only twice a week as opposed to daily.

Our class went on a memorable field trip to the Denver Museum of Art. We had worked with clay modeling and learned that a sculpture of a person's head and shoulders is called a bust. At the Museum, when we came into the room with all the busts, Reggie looked around in amazement and mused, "Wow, look at all these busses." The children enjoyed the museum. They observed a famous nude in the museum called "Linda," a life-like sculpture of a woman lying asleep on a table. They kept telling her to wake up. This was a day that I wanted to rescind my resignation, for sure.

When we returned to the center from the museum trip, as the children rested I thought of more ways to enrich their classroom learning environment. It didn't take me long to realize what was missing in the classroom—animals. In other schools where I had taught, I brought animals into the classroom so the children could study zoology. I have had up to four or five animals in different classifications . . . fish, bird, amphibian, reptile, and mammal. I remember when Rafael had come to me stuttering and pointing to the carpeted floor, "Linda, that alligator is out of his cage." He was referring to our class newt, which had climbed up the side of the aquarium and crawled out and onto the floor. Then there was the time some years back when I asked my class to name a mammal and Erin had answered, "Dolly Parton is a mammal." Next week I would go out and get some birds for the children to care for and observe. I thought birds or fish would be easier to begin with and maybe we could add more later. So birds it would be.

It would have been nice if someone had told me about the parakeet problem before I brought the birds into the child development center.

Only after I purchased them did I learn that parakeets can carry disease and are not approved for classroom settings. I decided, on a snowy afternoon, to return the birds to the department store where I had purchased them and get a pair of finches instead. On my way there, I stopped the car abruptly and the bird cage in the back seat toppled over. The door of the cage came open and the two panicked parakeets began to fly around in my car. I parked the car in a bus lane on one of the busiest downtown streets. Eventually, I caught both birds and placed them back into the cage. After wrapping a blanket over the cage, I ran the parakeets into the store, leaving the car parked in the bus lane. I emerged with two gentle finches and managed to get back to my car before it was towed.

When I returned to the child development center, I had feathers all over my hair and a somewhat crazed look on my face. But in the cage were a darling little male and female finch that would later mate and have babies in the cage and provide us with the central focus in the classroom that year. The children were able to watch the father finch gather yarn and nesting materials from the bottom of the cage and prepare the nest for the mother. The kindergartners watched the new babies grow and observed the family dynamics of Mr. and Mrs. Finch and their babies.

Plants and new growth have been a metaphor for me in my teaching career. Green plants symbolize birth and new beginnings. They project a promise that everything will be all right, and that everything is, in fact, all right now, in this moment. And it was the sight of little plants that signaled a shift for me that year.

I was going through so much stress in this job at the child development center that the last thing on my mind was cleaning out my car. One day, for some reason, I removed the mat on the floor in the back of my car behind the driver's seat. And what did I see? A little yellowish-green field of sprouts growing in the floor covering. The bird seed in the parakeet cage must have spilled when the cage flipped over weeks before and I had inadvertently provided moisture each time I scraped snow from my car and left the wet snow scraper on the mat. And just enough sunlight had filtered through my car windows to help the seeds grow into plants. I took this as a good sign. Everything would be all right.

The enrollment at that center had grown. We had begun the process of transforming the other centers in this agency into Montessori learning environments—child-centered classrooms packed with opportunities for students to engage in purposeful hands-on projects, using language and mathematics, and to learn independence and self-sufficiency. We were written up in the newspaper. Women in the community were granted scholarships and trained in the Montessori philosophy of teaching.

This kind of emotional rollercoaster is common among those who teach. At the end of the day, we are exhausted. We feel as if we cannot teach another day—that is, until tomorrow. In the morning we find the strength to come back and teach again. Why? Because we love and believe in children. We behold the gifts in them and nurture the children to become their most magnificent selves. We hold on to hope that their futures will be bright and glorious. The day that we don't go back might well be the day that we miss the miracle of a child making a connection, saying something funny or profound, creating a work of art, and giving our lives meaning and purpose. We must return because the call resonates in a place deep within us, and we must answer, "Yes!"

The winter turned to spring, and I drove up to the Red Rocks Amphitheater for the Easter sunrise service. The Archbishop gave the sermon. In his speech, he quoted the Archbishop Desmond Tutu, who once said, "I am a prisoner of hope." That quote moved me deeply. "I am a prisoner of hope." I could identify with that declaration. Hope has me just as teaching does.

On the way back home, I saw a sign at a home announcing the birth of miniature lop-eared bunnies. They were for sale. I turned off the road to the house and bought our class a new bunny. I named him Desmond, for Bishop Tutu. Desmond became the mascot for the Mile High Northeast Montessori Center. He lived at the center during the week and at our home on the weekends. I heard through the grapevine that word got back to Archbishop Tutu in South Africa that there was a lop-eared bunny rabbit in Denver, Colorado, named in his honor.

## REFLECTION

Why some people think teaching is an easy job, I will never understand. We work hard and make fools of ourselves so that children will be happy, learn, and grow. Every day is not one of inspiration and the pondering of noble thoughts. Many days leave us frustrated, drained, and unappreciated. It is a sweet indulgence when I give myself permission to lean into my emotions and even schedule nervous breakdowns. But in the morning, with the rising of the sun comes new hope, new joy, and the will to teach again.

As you think about the material in this chapter, ask yourself the following questions:

- Would you say that you chose the teaching profession or do you think it chose you? Do you feel that becoming a teacher was your destiny? Explain.

- Does the stress of your job ever get to you? What do you do to regain your passion and excitement for teaching when you're feeling down?

- What do you think Desmond Tutu meant when he said "I am a prisoner of hope"? Can you relate to this statement?

- What would you say to a young person who is considering a career as a teacher? What advice would you give that person about staying the course during the difficult times?

Ben and his sister Tarika perform an enchanting Thai dance.

## CHAPTER NINE

# Catch That Monk, He's Falling

*"As I am so freely forgiven, freely I forgive."*

"Why were we born?" the Buddhist monk asked the children. Before they could answer, he answered his own question. "We were born to practice goodness and gratitude to those around us."

Ben's mother, Eed, a native of Thailand, had invited the monk to our classroom. Everyone was excited because Eed had been coming into our classroom to help us learn about her country and Ben's heritage. The professional library delivered baskets of books on Thailand appropriate for kindergarten to third grade, and Eed and I planned a classroom celebration of the Thai new year, Songkran, which is celebrated in April, the month of the ending of the old and the coming of the new year, according to Thai belief.

The students read, wrote, and did art projects about Thailand. We made water lanterns and decorated the classroom with streamers and paper flowers. I went to a store that specialized in party decorations and purchased the most beautiful, colorful paper plates, matching napkins, plastic forks, and spoons available. Fresh flower arrangements of purple, red, yellow, pink, and orange made our luncheon table burst with color. A popular Thai restaurant in Denver catered our menu of Phat Thai fried noodles, Phat Kaphroa, which is meat stir fried with sweet basil, desserts, and beverages. Eed invited young women dressed in beautiful Thai clothing who performed traditional Thai dances. The children were delighted to see their classmate Ben and his older sister, Tarika, join in the dancing. Eed said that our Thai New Year celebration rivaled ones she had been to in Thailand. We were happy with the way the celebration had turned out. The only glitch had been that Eed had asked a Buddhist monk she knew to come for the celebration and he was unable to attend. Eed asked me if she could arrange to have him come at another time. I said that would be fine.

Eed continued to educate us about her country and its customs. She came to our classroom a few days before the monk was to visit to enlighten us on how to behave in the presence of a monk. The main point she emphasized was that no female is allowed to touch the monk. The boys were free to touch him, but the girls needed to keep their distance. I doubt that those little kindergarten girls even knew what a monk was, but it was the principle with which they took issue. Immediately, the girls started complaining that it was not fair. They wanted to know why the boys would get to touch the monk and they couldn't. Eed tried to explain that it was the religious tradition and that if a girl touched the monk he would be in trouble and have to say many prayers to be forgiven.

I had empowered my kindergarten students, especially the girls, to speak up and disagree when they think something is not right. I taught them early that they have a right to say no, to decline, to challenge ideas, and to respectfully disagree. It is my hope that my girls will remember these important life lessons as they mature into womanhood. Eed gave the explanation her best effort, but my girls were not buying it. In an attempt to solve the problem, I said, "Okay, okay, here is how we will do this. Nobody is going to touch the monk. Boys, girls, nobody. Can we all agree on that?" Everyone was fine with that.

Eed also taught us about the tradition of the hand water blessing. She told us she would bring in a brass bowl and a pitcher of scented water with rose petals. Eed would pour the rose water over our hands, clasped together as in prayer. This ritual symbolized respect, purification, and renewal. The blessing is used to wish a guest or friend good luck and prosperity. We thought this ritual sounded cool and we looked forward to having the monk come in and perform the hand water blessing with us.

The plan was for the monk to sit in a small wicker chair with a big, round back—a style that was popular in the '60s. To be on the safe side, I reviewed our agreement that no one would touch the monk. As a symbolic reminder, I drew a circle on the chalkboard with a slanted line through it. The children were quiet as they anticipated what this monk, whom no one was allowed to touch, would be like.

The monk arrived wearing his bright saffron robe. His kind aura permeated the room as he smiled and nodded lovingly, touching his palms together at his heart. Parents had come to join us in the classroom to meet the monk. Eed and I smiled and showed him over to the wicker chair. We didn't realize that the stability of the wicker chair had been compromised because of big adults sitting in it too often. Still smiling and bowing, the monk sat down and the wicker chair kept going backwards, spilling him onto the floor. All we could see were two little feet with white cotton socks and brown sandals kicking back and forth and his two hands flailing from side to side.

Eed and I screamed. All of our mother, nurturer, super-woman-to-the-rescue instincts kicked in at the same time and we rushed, with hands extended, to help the monk. After all those warnings to the children that no females could touch the monk, Eed and I thought nothing of reaching to grab his hands and pull him up from the floor. But the expression on the monk's face stopped us cold. What had first been a smiling, peaceful glow on the monk's face had turned into an angry snarl. We learned later that he was more worried about Eed and me touching him and having to say hundreds of prayers than any physical injury.

Two fathers of the kindergarten students rushed over and helped the monk to his feet. Eed and I backed away, staring, waiting to see what the monk would do next. Eed asked if he was all right. I was so glad the children did not laugh. They stayed seated "criss-cross-apple-sauce" on the carpeted flood with their hands over their mouths and eyes wide with concern. The monk nodded and rearranged his saffron robe until it was full length again. His peaceful smile returned, but he avoided the chair this time, choosing to deliver his speech standing. He began to speak of peace, kindness, love, understanding, and forgiveness, and Eed translated his words to the children.

"Don't have anger with your friend. Let go of anger. Love your friend," were his admonitions. He encouraged the children to work hard in school and he blessed each one by touching them on the head twice with a carnation that had been dipped in the rose water. The children enjoyed the splashing rose water blessing and no one touched the monk. Eed then poured the water with rose petals over the hands of the adults.

As the monk was leaving, I thanked him for visiting us. He did not charge a fee, but I thought it would be nice to give him a donation. I extended a check to him and I almost blew it again. The Monk could not even accept a piece of paper from my hand to his. He continued to smile and extended a natural, beige colored cotton bag and bowed. I dropped the check into his bag and the man from the temple who had come to drive him back to the monastery ushered him away. Cultural competence is an ongoing learning process, I thought to myself.

Weeks later Eed was at her temple and she asked the eldest monk how our visitor was doing. He sensed that her inquiry was more than just a casual courtesy and asked her why she seemed so bothered. When Eed recounted the story about him falling out of the chair, the eldest monk covered his mouth with his hand and laughed coyly. He told Eed that our monk had come back and not mentioned a word about his little mishap. Eed began to worry that she had let the cat out of the bag. Later that day she saw our monk. She told him that he was a very good sport about the whole incident. He said that he didn't know what it was with him and chairs. He shared with Eed that he had been speaking at the University of Thailand, and when he went on stage and sat down, he fell out of the chair in front of hundreds of students. Eed was relieved that he was not upset.

"Don't have anger with your friend. Let go of anger. Love your friend." I try to remember the monk's words as I teach each day and interact with parents, teachers, and administrators. There are certainly many opportunities to let those words of wisdom fall by the wayside and harbor anger and resentment over silly things. Here is a case in point.

The children and I were working on a big art project in the classroom. Time flies when you are having fun, and when I looked up at the clock, we had about three minutes to clean up the classroom and get ready to go to music class. I said to the children, "Wow, look at the time. Let's straighten up quickly so we can get to music class on time." Somewhere in that directive, Dajah and Amed interpreted my statement to mean, "Dajah and Amed, you stay behind in the classroom and finish cleaning while we go to the music room." I asked the children to form a line and routinely led them upstairs.

After dropping the children off at music, I took my extravagant bathroom break of the afternoon. After that I decided to go talk to the librarian about books for a special unit of study we were working on in my classroom. I never returned to the classroom until I collected the children from the music room. Two days later the principal called me in and told me that another teacher, who would remain anonymous, had told her that I left two children unsupervised in my classroom for 20 minutes. I had no idea what she was talking about. After investigating the situation, I found out that Daja and Amed had stayed in the classroom and continued to clean instead of joining the end of the line and going with us to music class. The anonymous teacher had asked Daja and Amed where their class had gone. They told her the students were at the music class, and she took them there while I was still in the library talking to the librarian. When I picked the children up from music class, Daja and Amed were with the other students and I did not realize that they had been brought in late.

No child had ever lagged behind for that period of time before. I thought the children understood that no one should ever be in the classroom alone. But because that big cleaning job was not finished, Daja and Amed decided to keep working until it was complete, even if it meant being in the classroom alone. My first reaction was to be very angry with the anonymous tattler. "Why couldn't she or he come to me and discuss this?" I asked my principal. I wondered how the teacher thought the principal would know why the children were in the room. Could this have been anything other than a mean-spirited attempt by this teacher to get me in trouble?

I demanded to know the secret identity of Mr. or Ms. Tattler. The principal refused to tell me, so I tracked the teacher down. I asked the two students who had found them in the classroom that day. They said they did not know her name, but they would recognize her if they saw her. We found her on the second floor. I put both my hands on my hips and told her a thing or two. I told her that I was a professional and that I would never intentionally leave students in the classroom by themselves. The next day, after I collected myself, I realized that this childish behavior on my part did not represent who I truly am, or who I strive to be.

"Don't have anger with your friend. Let go of anger. Love your friend." The monk's words echoed in my head. "We were born to practice goodness and gratitude to those around us." I had thought of myself as a very forgiving person. But I realized that forgiveness must be practiced regularly. I forgave the big things, which forced me to look at the situation and make a conscious choice to forgive. I thought of the time when I chose to forgive someone for calling me a "negress" and saying that my gorgeous, salon-maintained locks looked like they could be used to mop up the floor. That really hurt—and these words were delivered in church, of all places. But I forgave the man's ignorance. For me, it is those silly little day-to-day offenses that I harbor so that, in the words of my favorite poet, Langston Hughes, they "sag like a heavy load." It was not a time to be angry and hold a grudge.

As the Monk had taught me, I became willing to love my friend and to practice goodness and gratitude. I had brought fresh roses into our classroom that day for the children to arrange and beautify their learning environment. I pulled three roses from a vase on the table where I was sitting. I suggested to Daja and Amed that we write letters to the teacher who had been kind enough to take care of them and walk them up to music class. They wrote letters expressing their gratitude and made beautiful illustrations. In my letter to the teacher, I apologized for my rudeness. I thanked her for caring about my students and for going out of her way to help them. I, too, illustrated my letter with a pretty bad representation of a dove holding out an olive branch in its mouth and I sent the two students up to the teacher's room.

After Daja and Amed delivered the letters and roses to the teacher, she came to my classroom, cried, and thanked us. The air had been cleared, and I no longer felt anger in the pit of my stomach. Love was present. I reviewed the rule with the children that no one should ever stay behind alone anywhere and that we all must stay together.

## REFLECTION

I teach the children social skills and how to forgive each other, therefore I try to practice those skills myself. When they apologize to each other, I ask them to do it with genuine feeling and sincerity when they are ready. I do not force an apology. We say please and thank-you, and we help each other. From time to time I ask myself if I am practicing what I preach. It is my belief that people are doing the best they can in any given moment. When someone hurts us, it is usually nothing personal, really it's not. We all need to be loved and appreciated. It could have been that reporting this incident to the principal was this teacher's way of saying, "I care about the safety of the children at this school and I want you to love and appreciate me because of this." I tried, after I cooled down, to see the good in this situation. When I thought about it, the teacher had really helped me. Without the knowledge that the children had stayed in the classroom, Daja and Amed or other children might have done the same thing again. The lesson from the monk was simple, yet profound. Practice goodness, gratitude, and love each other.

As you think about the material in this chapter, ask yourself the following questions:

🪷 Have you ever had visitors to your classroom whose customs differed from those you and your students were used to? How did you prepare the students for such visits?

🪷 When you are upset with someone at your school or in your life, what steps do you take to let go of your anger? Have you shared such strategies with your students?

🪷 Have you ever become angry with a colleague and then discovered that there is another side to the story? What have you done to make amends with this colleague?

🪷 How do you think your students would interpret the monk's admonitions? Discuss these with your class: "Don't have anger with your friend. Let go of anger. Love your friend." How do your students typically resolve classroom conflicts?

A kindergartner reads an excerpt from Dr. Martin Luther King, Jr.'s, "I Have a Dream" speech.

## CHAPTER TEN

# Go With the Flow, Even If It's Pee

*"I dance to the rhythm of the lessons in life and everything I do turns out better than I planned it."*

৯৯

It was Lily's turn to read. She was so excited about reading excerpts from Dr. King's famous speeches to the entire school assembly that she had not gone to the bathroom, as I had requested, before she took center stage. In the middle of Lily's reading, I noticed her doing the "I need to go to the bathroom" wiggle. Sometimes I call it "the holding pattern." I would recognize it anywhere. I think the wiggle got worse around the part about "justice rushing down like waters and righteousness like a mighty stream." I walked up to the stage and whispered to Lily, "Do you need to go to the bathroom?" "Yes," she whispered back, this time with no protest. I held the microphone while Lily went to the bathroom. To fill the dead time, I led the audience in the song "Did You Feed My Cow?" ("Yes, m'am. Can you tell me how? Yes, m'am. What did you feed her? Corn and hay!") That was the first song that came to mind, I guess because Ella Jenkins does such a fabulous job of singing it in a call-and-response style. Later, I reflected that maybe I should have led the audience in "We Shall Overcome." Lily returned, relieved, refreshed, and ready to continue. (The interruption did not shake Lily one bit. Many children at the age of five are naturally and developmentally egocentric. Lily returned with confidence. It was as if she thought, "Of course the world should stop and wait for me. After all, I am the center of the universe, am I not?") She finished her reading to thunderous applause. Parents who were videotaping suggested that we send that footage to "America's Funniest Home Videos." We never did.

Contrary to what some people believe, educators included, most children are not shy or afraid to perform before large audiences. Or, I should say, my students are very confident in front of a crowd. We practice speaking, listening, and performance in the classroom every day. There are usually a few natural "stars" in any class who don't mind working a crowd. My experience has been that the children who are inclined to feel more self-conscious or shy will feed off the stars and a synergistic effect is unleashed. Leading off with the eager performers makes it easier for the shy ones to follow suit.

I must address the "high expectations" principle again. When I expect that all the children will enjoy performing, I get exactly what I expect, especially once the children get positive feedback and acknowledgement from their parents, principal, other teachers, and upper class students. They enjoy the attention and opportunity to flaunt their talents. If anything, we sometimes need that old-fashioned "hook" to get them off the stage! Lily's moment was another one of those daily occurrences where life just keeps on "life-ing" and all we can do is to go with life's flow. My objective as a teacher is not to create perfect experiences for my children, it is to help the children learn and have fun. I believe in the process, not just the product; the journey, not just the destination. It is this philosophy that enables me to stand fearless and take risks when teaching children. I believe that our so-called mistakes are actually opportunities for further growth. I have trusted children to cut vegetables with paring knives, wash real china dishes, fish at a lake, answer the telephone, and speak to a real, live judge in a court of law. I keep in mind that we must go with the proverbial flow—things don't always go as planned, but that's okay.

I selected Doreen Cronin's *Click, Clack, Moo: Cows That Type* as a read-aloud text. As a writing extension, I asked the children what they might want to request from our principal. (The cows in the book had requested electric blankets.) They discussed this question among themselves and came up with the answer: an ice cream and pizza party. The daily writing assignments became writing letters to the principal. I informed the principal of our latest writing project and asked for his cooperation. He agreed to deny the request and to keep the conversation going to encourage my kindergarten students to keep writing. The first letter composed by the kindergartners read:

*Dear Principal,*

*We are hungry here in our kindergarten classroom. We demand pepperoni pizza and ice cream sundaes.*

*Sincerely,*
*Ms. Alston's Class*

The exchange became very lively when the principal copped an attitude and wrote responses like:

*Dear Kindergarten Class and Ms. Alston,*

*Pizza and ice cream sundaes. No way, José! This is a school, not Pizza Hut or Dairy Queen.*

*Adamantly,*
*The Principal*

The principal wrote the letters back to the children on large, chart paper. I used his letters as our reading charts. We incorporated rich vocabulary like "adamantly" and "unwaveringly." The children couldn't wait until after lunchtime when we did our writing workshop to read what the principal had written to them. In *Click, Clack, Moo*, the cows threaten to go on strike and protest if their problem is not resolved. The children and I discussed our dilemma, and it was unanimous: We went on strike, refusing to read and write. Here is the paradox that was so cute. While the kindergartners went on strike from reading and writing, they were, in fact, doing more reading and writing than they had all school year. They were thrilled to write the principal letters informing him that they were on strike and read what he wrote in response.

*Dear Principal,*

*You leave us no choice. This is the ultimatum. If we do not have pizza in our classroom by three forty-five p.m. mountain standard time today, we will go on strike! We will not write another word. We will not illustrate another page.*

*Unyieldingly,*
*Ms. Alston's Class*

At three forty-five, no pepperoni pizza or ice cream had arrived in the kindergarten classroom. The principal fired back:

*Dear Ms. Alston's Class,*

*You are on strike? Well, take a hike! I believe this is extortion! This is a school. You are here to learn to be great writers. You have forced me to litigate.*

*Litigiously,*
*The Principal*

This exchange went on for about two weeks. The children were having a ball, and I had never seen the principal happier. One day he was stressed out with administrative matters and had an office filled with students who had been sent to him for misbehaving. He glanced up and noticed an interesting sight through his office door. My students and I were marching past his office in protest. Each student had written and decorated a sign. Some signs read, "Pizza and ice cream now!" My sign demanded Dr. Atkins' sugar-free ice cream and Diet Coke. The principal shared with me later that our timing for the strike was perfect because he was at his wit's end that day and the interruption was just what he needed. He tried to maintain his staunch, annoyed demeanor, but those adorable little giggling kindergartners with their protest signs were too much for him. Through his laughter he admonished us, "Return to class at once and continue reading and writing!"

Meanwhile, serendipity graced us again. It just so happened that Jalen's father was a city councilman. He had invited me to bring our class to visit him at the brand new city offices and courthouse, but I had not considered taking the class on this field trip until it aligned with our writing project. I contacted Jalen's father and asked if the offer still stood to bring the children to the courthouse and he said that it did. The students and I wrote another letter to the principal. We expressed that it was regrettable that it had come to this, but he had left us no choice but to litigate. We were taking him to court.

Later that week, Jalen's father "served" the principal with a summons to appear in court. Jalen's dad arranged with an African-American judge to schedule our class for the trial against the principal. The judge was very excited about participating in our project. I sent a script to His Honor outlining what I wanted him to say, and a copy of *Click, Clack, Moo*. I asked him to emphasize the vocabulary words we had studied. He agreed to let the children testify, and his verdict would be that the court would provide the pizza there at the courthouse and he would order our principal to provide ice cream back at the school. This, I felt, was a fair verdict because anyone could clearly see that the principal was as wrong as two left shoes.

When we arrived at the courthouse, the judge was finishing up a case. He said, "Now that I have completed these trivial proceedings, I will turn my attention to a matter of great importance. It is the matter of case number 1-2-3-4-5, Ms. Alston's kindergarten class vs. the principal." The judge was absolutely brilliant. He handled that case with all the professionalism, legalese, and protocol of a real court hearing. He had our letters entered as exhibits and he had the bailiff swear in each child. There were two students with the same last name as the judge's. When he questioned them, the judge established that they did not know each other before that day and that they were in no way related.

The principal was ill that day so the assistant principal testified in his behalf. Her argument was that the school could not provide pizza and ice cream because of the danger that some children might be lactose intolerant. She added that the school served healthy meals during breakfast and lunch and was not required to feed the students additional pizza. Further, she argued that the administration did not want to contribute to the epidemic of obesity among our young school children today by giving the children unnecessary or inappropriate food. It was obvious that the judge was a little biased in our favor. He asked the assistant principal to look over into the jury box where my kindergarten students were bouncing up and down on the cushioned seats. He asked her if any of those children looked obese to her. She had to answer "no." The judge then asked the assistant principal if she had proof that any of my kindergarten children had a medical condition known as "lactose intolerance." He had her cornered again.

But the assistant principal had prepared well and did not come to court to play around. She had presented a compelling defense. There is, in fact, a problem with obesity among young children in our society and some children *are* lactose intolerant. I was impressed that she had planned so well and presented her case so seriously. Of course, she was just going along with the plan. In reality, she and the principal, as well as the parents and visitors who accompanied us, knew that eating extra pizza and ice cream was not a frequent practice in my classroom. They were all aware that I had a healthy food policy in my classroom and some had tasted the organic sprouts we grew and ate—they knew this would just be a tasting of pizza and ice cream.

The judge ruled in our favor. After he rendered his decision, he asked if we had any questions. The children asked questions such as why he wanted to become a judge. Some parents asked questions as well. Then came one of those "go with the flow" moments. Desiree asked the judge if it was wrong for a man to cheat on a woman. The judge was a little embarrassed by the question but handled it well. He said, "Cheating is never a good thing for anyone to do to anyone else." Desiree's mom was divorced and had recently remarried. Obviously, Desiree had overheard conversations about infidelity.

Jalen's father wanted to make the visit as much fun as possible. He tried to think of everything he could do that the children would enjoy. He was able to arrange for a fire truck to come and park outside the courthouse, which was near a lake. The fire truck had nothing to do with the theme of the book or the court case, but it was great fun. The four firefighters turned on the water from the fire truck and allowed each child to hold the hose and feel the power of the water bursting forth. We were going with the flow.

Jalen's father paid for the pizza and made sure it came at the approximate time we were coming out of the court house. We ate pizza beside the beautiful lake, with ducks, flowers, and trees on that gorgeous spring day.

Two days later, back at the school I delivered ice cream and toppings to the principal's office and gave him the opportunity to admit his defeat and obey the judge's ruling. The two days between the court date and the day of the ice cream treat gave the principal a chance to feel better. It also showed sensitivity to the assistant principal's concern about obesity in our youth. I already knew that none of the children were lactose intolerant because of medical questionnaires that parents had filled out at the beginning of the school year. The principal brought the ice cream to our classroom. The children cheered. They had taken him to task and won their case. They had learned to use and spell big, impressive words and to write complex, persuasive arguments. Imani laughed as she licked ice cream from her spoon. She said, "We gave the principal a good ultimatum."

## REFLECTION

There are popular bumper stickers that read, "I'd Rather Be Sailing," "I'd Rather Be Biking," or "I'd Rather Be Skiing." I like the one I saw that said, "I'd Rather Be Here Now." The more we choose life the way it is right here, right now, the more peace and joy becomes available to us. Serendipity seeks us out and aligns circumstances and events to cause miraculous outcomes, beyond our wildest imaginings.

As you think about the material in this chapter, ask yourself the following questions:

- Have you ever deflected a potentially embarrassing situation for a student in your classroom? Explain.

- Can you think of something your students might like to request of the principal at your school? In addition to writing letters, what are some strategies students can use to make their case?

- Do you "go with the flow" in your teaching? What are the risks of doing this in the classroom? What are the advantages?

- Describe a time in your class when an unexpected development led to an outcome that surpassed your wildest imaginings.

On June 14th, 2006, the Rocky Mountain News printed a story with this photo and caption, "Linda Alston, winner of the Kinder Excellence in Teaching Award, celebrates the announcement Tuesday. Talking in her right ear is Mary Ann Bash, the Denver Public Schools teacher who nominated her; talking in her left ear is college friend Tyrone Wilson."

CHAPTER ELEVEN

# $100,000 Teacher

*"I embrace each experience on my journey and
know that all is well."*

I did not choose teaching. Teaching chose me. Are we all born with the proverbial "blank canvas" upon which we paint our destiny? Or do we come to the planet with our paths already charted out? Most mornings when I wake up I certainly like to think that I have free will in life to choose and to make my own decisions. However, I realize that my choices are driven and influenced by situations and circumstances in my background, such as race, culture, gender, geography, family history, education, physical attributes, marital status, and possibly what cycle the moon is in or whether Mercury is in retrograde. Was it written somewhere in permanent marker that I was born to be a teacher? Was it predestined? Did I have a choice? What would have happened if I had pursued acting or psychology, pottery making or dance? Billy Dee Williams and I could have been old pals for years by now. I might have been in practice with Dr. Alvin Poussaint. I could be the artistic director of my own art boutiques that house my exquisite sculptures or I could have danced with Alvin Ailey and Judith Jamison.

But every time I went looking for other professions, all roads led me back to teaching. I would go to apply for the job of administrative assistant and the person in human resources would say, "Sorry, that position has been filled, however, I know about a teaching job you might be interested in across town at the Head Start program." I would sit there and wonder how we got from my working there in that office to working across town at the Head Start program. This much I know is true: In the words of author and poet Maya Angelou, "I wouldn't take nothing for my journey now."

The journey began when I was a young girl about the age of 12 growing up in Louisiana. Elder J. H. Feltus, the pastor of my church, had a habit of assigning the young girls to teach Sunday school to the little children. As I recall, I think this would happen when the real Sunday school teacher was absent and he didn't have anyone else. We had no time for advance preparation. He would simply look out into the congregation and say, "Sister Lindy [that was me] will teach the young people's class today." That was the end of that story. Clearly a case where there was no choice in the matter. My girlfriends and I would try to put our heads down or pretend we were picking up a church bulletin that had fallen on the floor so Elder Feltus would not spot us and arbitrarily give us the assignment. Sometimes it worked and sometimes it didn't.

Neither my friends nor I liked teaching the little children, but each time I did teach them it was blessed. The children became very excited about their learning. I don't remember any Sunday school manuals to follow like the ones the church started to use later. I had to make up the lesson off the top of my head and remember some of what I had learned in my own Sunday school class for teenagers.

It was not long before Elder Feltus made me the permanent teacher for the class. What captured my interest and caused me to like teaching the Sunday school class was the way the children became excited about learning. That was cool. I noticed that I had a skill for being able to break down the advanced, sophisticated concepts I was hearing from other teachers into words and ideas that my little children could grasp. The children were performing like biblical scholars and loving their Sunday school class. Suddenly, my friends who, like me, had not wanted to teach the little children were trying to undermine me for the coveted position. The job had now become attractive.

Elder Feltus and the church mother, Mother Norman, were impressed by the new enthusiasm for Sunday school they witnessed in my students. But as a teenager I would get tired of having to teach every Sunday. One Sunday I told my mother flat out that I was not going, period. When my mother and Sister Phoebe returned home from church later that day, they brought me little gifts the children had made for me along with a gift from the church that Mother Norman had purchased for me. The Sunday I chose to skip teaching was the very Sunday they were going to show their appreciation for me for doing such an outstanding job as their teacher. I felt terrible that I had missed out on that.

This was a powerful lesson that has stayed with me ever since. It seems that we experience the strongest urge to quit a difficult experience just before the miracle happens, the rewards are reaped, and the victory is won. Two of the boys in my class turned out to be ministers and a couple of girls became missionaries, so I guess I didn't confuse them too much.

My mother taught Head Start in the summers, and while I was home from college, there was nothing else to do in my little town, so I went with her to the Head Start program. There was no air conditioning in those rooms and the temperature was burning hot. But I enjoyed working with the children. Head Start was very comprehensive. It included academics, nutrition, parent education, recreational activities, and health. I think my worst moment there occurred the day the children had to bring in a bowel movement specimen in a little jar that would be sent out to a lab and tested for diseases and worms. The jars had been sent home with a tongue depressor stick in the bag for the parents to use to place the stool specimen into the jar. Some parents had included the used stick in the bag with the jar when they returned it.

This was one day my attraction to teaching could have died a violent death, never again to be resurrected. But this was also the day that my cousin Hydria Jean-Baptiste, himself an educator and administrator in the program, said something to me that would come back to haunt me later in life. Hydria had noticed my natural teaching skills while I was working with the children. He asked me the day the stool specimens were returned what I was planning to major in at Howard University. I told him psychology. He looked down into my eyes and in his deep southern drawl said slowly, "Linda, don't miss your calling."

While at Howard University I majored in African-American studies and sociology, and I took some education courses because my boyfriend told me that education courses were good to have in case nothing else worked out in terms of a career. Teaching would be something to, as he put it, "fall back on."

After getting married and having three sons of my own, I became interested in my children's education. I began taking education courses and received Wisconsin state certification and an AMI Montessori degree. And each time I taught a class of students, they excelled and I loved it. But it never seemed that I should really be a teacher. It all seemed to me just a temporary chain of events, and that I would be something else when I really grew up. Teaching was just the proverbial dress rehearsal.

My initial reluctance to teach was reinforced by attitudes around me. What a low value people place on teaching and how little appreciation they have for what I now consider the noblest of professions! A former classmate, who went into politics once said to me, "Linda, you went to Howard University and got all these degrees JUST to become a teacher? You could have stayed in Louisiana and done that." People can be so cruel, can't they? It was never that I thought teaching was beneath me or of lesser value than other jobs. I just couldn't see myself doing it, in much the same way I could not see myself being a doctor because I would faint at the sight of blood. My classmate's comment caused me to question once again why I was a teacher.

But little by little, and then by quantum leaps, my confirmation came that teaching is my life's calling—or maybe I chose to lean in, embrace it, and declare it so. Whichever one it was, free will or destiny, teaching was mine. It had me. I can remember the exact moment that I "got it" that I was going to be a teacher and how many wonderful blessings had come to me through teaching already. I was in a hotel conference room in Chicago attending a personal growth seminar that had nothing to do with teaching. I was sharing thoughts with a woman named Lillian about how I wanted to work my way into something else besides teaching. Her response was, "I don't know, Linda. You have traveled to Africa. I haven't been out of the country." Lillian was a successful financial planner in Chicago, yet she was reminding me that teaching had given me the gift of being a Fulbright Scholar and afforded me the opportunity of visiting the West African country of Sierra Leone. In that moment, the gifts that had been given to me because I was a teacher flooded over me. It was just as people say: "my life flashed before me." I could see faces of children I had taught, heard phrases the children had said when something I had taught them had clicked, recalled thank-yous from parents, laughter, joy, and tears. It was as if, in that moment, I truly chose to be a teacher, and my life has never been the same.

In 1987 I moved to Denver, Colorado. It was not long before I was teaching in public, private, and charter schools again. And pretty soon, the awards and accolades came flowing in. The first teaching award I received was the Edward F. Calesa "Terrific Teachers Making A Difference Award." It was a new award that recognized excellence in teaching. I had never heard of it. I did not even know anyone had recommended me for it, but one day I received a letter in the mail saying that I was a recipient. Other Colorado teachers and I were honored with a $500 stipend to be used for a school project, and we were invited to a mountain resort and treated royally for a weekend. It was lovely, but it was only the beginning.

Subsequently, I was recognized for excellence in teaching with the following honors: the National Council of Negro Women's Excellence in Teaching Award, Walt Disney American Teacher Award (finalist), Milken National Educator Award, Denver Distinguished Teacher Award, the Mary McCleod Bethune Legacy Award, and the Denver Links, Inc. Dr. Albert C. Yates Educator Award.

But being a teacher has it heartaches, too. Often the award-winning teacher is not recognized or appreciated in her own country so to speak, meaning her school building. I hear stories of teachers who strive for excellence and innovation in their teaching only to be ostracized and left to have lunch alone. What has been extremely painful in the teaching profession is that while many of my colleagues applaud and encourage my quest for high ideals and excellence, some of my fellow teachers and administrators seem to work against me and deliberately try to make my professional life "h-e-double hockey sticks." I have heard many exemplary teachers express this same regret.

I asked a friend, who was a school custodian, what she thought I did to make some of the teachers envy or dislike me. "I don't try to run anything around here," I said. "I don't try to tell other teachers what to do or how to run their classrooms. I am more than willing to share what I know when I can. I don't drive a Jaguar or wear fancy clothes and jewels. Most days find my face bare with no makeup. I am not the most beautiful, thin, rich person in the building. What is it about me that would cause anyone to be jealous? I just try to do the very best job I possibly can for the children in my classroom. Don't teachers want all of us to give the best we have to the children?" Her answer was this. She said, "Linda, you have a dignity and certainty about who you are that is unshakeable. You don't think any more or less of yourself no matter who you are with. People don't like that sometimes. It's not about clothes and diamonds and cars. It's about personal dignity."

The school year 2004–2005 was a living nightmare. In previous years, the principal had worshipped the ground I walked on. I could do no wrong. This particular year, I couldn't do anything right. This was the year I named the "Year of Maybe."

The year started off on an ominous note. On the first day of school, before the children had even entered the building, I was already exhausted from setting up the learning environment. One of my kindergarteners that year was a little girl named Daisy, who was what we call a runner. When Daisy's mom or dad attempted to leave her in the classroom, she would bolt out the door after them. I was alone in the room with the children until the paraprofessional came an hour later, so when Daisy took off, I was faced with a dilemma. I could run out of the room after her and leave 24 children alone in the room. Or, I could stay with the class and hope that Daisy was with her parent and hadn't found her way to the street and into the path of a Mack truck.

Daisy's parents complained to the principal that I was a cold, uncaring teacher because I would not run after their daughter. Never mind the fact that their little Daisy was out of control and they could not make her listen and stay in the classroom when they left. The principal took their side in a very unprofessional way. He yelled at me for not running out of the building after Daisy, and everything else I did that year. The assistant principal would hide in the hallway that divided my room and the other kindergarten classroom to try to listen for something that I was doing wrong. This was by far the worst year of my teaching career . . . maybe. At the end of that year, I knew I had to leave the school. I could not understand what was happening to this illustrious career of mine.

I accepted a kindergarten teaching position at a school that some considered to be the poorest in the state of Colorado. I chose to go to the school because it was also one of the most diverse communities in the school district and I thought these children could benefit most from my teaching expertise. This school was the biggest challenge of my entire teaching career. It had beaten out the last school for this dubious distinction. The behavior problems were extreme and the community was plagued with far too many social and economic ills to mention. But the children thrived in my classroom. The order and consistency of our rituals and routines gave them something constant in their lives, and in this environment, they were able to learn and grow. They excelled in reading and even advanced mathematics, such as multiplication and geometry.

One day in December, a friend who is a literacy coach called me about an announcement for a teaching award called the Kinder Excellence In Teaching Award (the first word is pronounced like the first part of "kindergarten"). The award would be given to K–12 teachers, and the caption read, "If a doctor, lawyer, or business person can earn more than $100,000 in one year, why not a teacher?" The teacher who received this award would receive $100,000, an unrestricted amount of money for the teacher's personal use. She or he could decide to use it for any purpose. At first I thought my friend misunderstood something about this award. This could not be possible, that someone would just up and give a teacher $100,000. I read the announcement myself. It explained that Rich and Nancy Kinder of Houston, Texas, along with KIPP (Knowledge Is Power Program), an organization dedicated to building college-preparatory public schools, wanted to bring attention to the value of teachers in order to emphasize the need for higher pay.

Another friend of mine, Mary Ann Bash, decided to nominate me. Mary Ann had followed my teaching career for more than 13 years. She had collected an archive of newspaper articles, statistics, programs, videos, and other artifacts that illustrated my professional accomplishments. Mary Ann often spontaneously breaks into a story about a great teaching moment in my career. When the story comes to the punch line, she turns to me with both hands pointing in my direction. That is my cue to deliver one of my famous quotes. The problem is, I never remember what she is even talking about! Every teacher in the world should have a dear, loyal, adoring friend like Mary Ann. She quickly takes to task anyone who would dare say they are my biggest fan. "You must be number two, because I am number one," she chides.

Mary Ann submitted the nomination on February 1. A few weeks later, I was notified that I had been selected as one of ten finalists. This was a great honor and wonderful thing . . . maybe! I also learned that Catherine North, from the Kinder Excellence In Teaching Award program, would be coming to observe me teaching all day for two days. I was panic stricken. The idea that someone, anyone, was coming to observe me teaching for two entire days was one thing, but that $100,000 was riding on it seemed too much to bear. I am not the kind of teacher who can show off what I do and how I teach. I prefer that the results of my teaching be shown in the knowledge and behavior of the children. But Catherine North was coming, and I had to be ready for her.

Mary Ann and I expected Ms. North to be an older woman with many years of experience. In walked a young, beautiful, unpretentious woman, but one who was the consummate professional. Older women with decades of experience could learn a thing or two from Catherine. I had never met anyone so professional and objective. We couldn't offer her a cup of coffee without her refusing so as to avoid it being some kind of conflict of interest.

I realized that there was nothing for me to do but to be myself and go with the flow of the day as I always do. On the first morning of my observation, the father of one of my students came into the classroom and told us about how he had been shot at his job. There were interruptions and fire drills and assemblies all day long. Parents came in and out. At one point, I noticed my little student, Tiffany, standing and reading what Catherine was writing as she took copious notes. Catherine was apparently jotting notes in shorthand and was not concerning herself with punctuation. Tiffany pointed out to Catherine that she needed a period after a certain sentence.

Was this site visit going well . . . maybe? The children acted out, but were also their sweet, adorable selves. It was just another day in the life of my classroom. At the end of the second day, Catherine North interviewed me and that concluded the observation.

Soon after, Annette Espanoza from the *Denver Post* came to my classroom and wrote an article that took front-page color coverage, as my son Joshua the journalist would say, "above the fold." Was this a good thing? Maybe! I was self-conscious about having my picture in the paper and worried what the article would say. My classroom was very dynamic, and the children were engaged in all sorts of activities. I didn't know what any given student might have done or said when Annette observed them during independent work. The weeks flew by and the school year ended. Mary Ann and I would have to wait for the results, which we were told would be announced in June.

And wouldn't you know, in mid-June, Mary Ann and I were flown to Washington, D C. We thought all the finalists were going to be there, but it was just the two of us, and on June 13, 2006, I was awarded the first-ever Kinder Excellence In Teaching Award and a check for $100,000. Rich and Nancy Kinder were at the press conference. So was KIPP co-founder Mike Feinberg, and other members of the blue ribbon panel of judges who had chosen me, a kindergarten teacher. Margaret Spellings, the United States secretary of education, presented the award to me. Was this a good and glorious thing? Maybe! I had to give interviews for television, radio, and magazines and make speeches. I am really a very shy person and prefer to keep under the radar. But with this great honor and generous, unprecedented gift there was no chance of that. Was this a good thing? You better believe it!

Most people could not believe that the $100,000 was for me personally. They kept referring to it as "that grant," meaning that I had to use it for research or some other school-related project. But that money was mine, all mine. Everybody asked what I would do with the money, but for a while I was floating around in a state that I called "clinically diagnosable shock" so I could not think about it. When I did start letting my imagination go, the first thing that came into my head was orange geraniums. I had been very positional, or as my friend Sherry and I say, "additudinal," about these geraniums that summer because they cost more than the pink and red ones. I had refused to buy them even though I loved the color. It was the principle. But after I received that big check, I thought, "What the heck? I'll spurge!"

After I bought the geraniums, I basically did what my financial advisor told me to do regarding investments and savings, and paid off my midnight blue, previously owned Toyota Camry. My other fantasy was to go to Martha's Vineyard to meet Carly Simon and hear her sing. It is a good thing to know influential people. Andrea Dukakis of Colorado Public Radio got word to Carly Simon that I wanted to hear her sing. One day I answered my phone and a beautiful, melodious voice said, "Linda, this is Carly Simon." As she played the guitar, she sang the two songs I requested: "Coming Around Again" and "Jesse" (my all-time favorite). Then she chose to add

> " . . . you're a legend in your own time
>
> A hero in the footlights
>
> Playin' tunes to fit your rhyme . . ."

## REFLECTION

The saying goes that it is all right to talk to yourself but you're in trouble when you start to answer back. However, when I find myself asking the questions over and over—"Why am I being treated this way? I've done nothing but try to do my job in excellence. Why is this happening to me?"—I have to remind myself that I am right. I haven't done anything to deserve cruel treatment. Therefore, maybe the experiences are there to thrust me forward and toward my highest good. I have been blessed with numerous accolades as a teacher. But there have also been times when this recognition has been accompanied by ostracism and contempt. It has all made me stronger and a little wiser. Finally, I understand that people are going to think what they want of you no matter what you do.

Many teachers go through this valley when they begin to receive recognition. I say to you, stand strong! Hold your moral high ground. Keep giving your all, for the children. Otherwise, you will not be able to face yourself in the mirror. The very acts that people do against you can work out in your favor in a mighty way. No one can block that which is rightfully yours and mine. Look at your whole journey and be overcome with gratitude, gladness, and praise. Draw strength and tenacity from the words of Marianne Williamson:

> Our deepest fear is not that we are inadequate. Our deepest fear is that we are powerful beyond measure. It is our light, not our darkness that most frightens us. We ask ourselves, Who am I to be brilliant, gorgeous, talented, fabulous? Actually, who are you not to be? . . . Your playing small does not serve the world. There is nothing enlightened about shrinking so that other people won't feel insecure around you. We are all meant to shine, as children do. It's not just in some of us; it's in everyone. And as we let our own light shine, we unconsciously give other people permission to do the same. As we are liberated from our own fear, our presence automatically liberates others.

As you think about the material in this chapter, ask yourself the following questions:

- What made you become a teacher? Do you ever question this decision? What do you do to remind yourself of why you chose this noble profession?

- What do you think Maya Angelou meant when she wrote "I wouldn't take nothing for my journey now?" Have you gone through challenging periods in your life and career that turned out to be important turning points?

- Have you ever received accolades or awards for your teaching? Describe any positive or negative impacts you experienced as a result of this recognition.

- Have you ever felt that a colleague or administrator was trying to undermine your professional life? How did you cope with that situation? What can you do to encourage your colleagues to be the best teachers they can be?

Think kindergartners can't learn multiplication?
Believe they can, teach them, and they will!

## CHAPTER TWELVE

# Linda's Teaching Secrets Revealed

*"I take action now, I achieve astonishing results, and I know*
*that I know that I know!"*

This is the end of my book so I've got to "bring it" now. The experiences that I have shared with you can be accomplished by all teachers and children, anywhere, and at any time. The ideas embedded in my stories are not "don't try this at home" stunts. Whether it is teaching a young child to read before large audiences, using sophisticated vocabulary, contemplating issues of culture and race, interviewing dignitaries or serving tea with fine china, these skills are achievable and authentic.

The following are my three fundamental principles, which serve as the foundation of my success:

**Believe in the child!** Many say they believe in the child. But in the next breath, both teachers and parents alike tell me they would never trust a child to handle fine china, care for plants and animals, or speak and perform. To them I say, "Where then is your belief laid bare?" If you believe the child can read, let them read for Pete's sake! Do not withhold learning for fear that it is too much, will damage the brain, or is too sophisticated. So what if the children are poor, of color, white, wealthy and sheltered, or "ghetto fabulous!" Make no excuses! Make learning fun. I am often challenged because I teach young children to read passages like: "Our deepest fear is not that we are inadequate. Our deepest fear is that we are powerful beyond measure . . ." by Marianne Williamson. People tell me the children don't have the comprehension. To them I say, "maybe." That's where I come in. I teach it to them. Good old-fashioned direct instruction. But if you believe in children, that they have something to offer to you, to each other, and to the world, you will be absolutely floored by the insights young children will express on a passage like the Williamson one. Choose one of your favorite poems or passages. Sit down with a child. Read it to him or her. Teach that child to read it. Open up a discussion and watch what will happen. I double dare you! You will be calling people all over the country quoting what the child said. That's a promise.

Back to the comprehension argument. Children don't comprehend that today is Thursday or the month is June either, the whole space-time continuum thing. Does that stop us from teaching them the days of the week and months of the year? We are scaffolding a foundation of knowledge, ideas, images, and ongoing inquiry. I don't understand electricity. But I understand it well enough to know that when I plug in my blender, the blades will turn and I get a smoothie. George Benson's song, "The Greatest Love of All" always moves us. It begins, "I believe that children are our future. Teach them well and let them lead the way." Sometimes I think we make camp at the "children are our future" and "teach them well" parts and forget to journey on to "let them lead the way."

**Do it!** In *The Wizard of Oz,* one of my favorite children's stories by L. Frank Baum, Dorothy believed that she could get home to Kansas. But she had to take action, she had to DO stuff. She had to follow the yellow-brick road and take out the Wicked Witch of the West. My girl was unstoppable! Along the way she found friends of the same ilk who believed in something they wanted for themselves. They joined her on her adventure. Surround yourself with others who believe in children and will demand excellence. Try some of my ideas. Think of what inspires you that you would like to do in your classroom.

Don't worry that no one else is doing it. Don't worry what others will say when you know that what you are doing is for the highest good of the children. Newsflash! They're talking about you anyway. There is no way you can make them stop—they don't matter. But you have your self-expression and magnificence to lose if you back down—and that is a lot at stake! Suspend your fear of being excellent. Be your own brand. Think the entire lesson plan through. Put in every little detail of how you should teach it so that the children can do it successfully and independently. The secret is that it should be something that you love. Something that will make you spring out of bed in the morning to get to school and share it with the children. Do it now, because now is all there is. I've got on my glittery red pumps (gotta have that glitter). I'm clicking my heels three times for you.

**Catch sight of your results!** Celebrate your victories with the students, both great and small. Chronicle your own stories and successes. Don't wait for someone else to acknowledge your work. Encourage yourself. Stand in your power and greatness. Define yourself. Apologize to no one for who you are. Modesty is often the ego in disguise, and it's highly overrated. Share your successes and joys with the parents of your students.

Document your students' progress in anecdotal notes, video and audio recordings, and artifacts of the students' work. Show off the children's talents and abilities. Do not listen to people who put teachers down. Tell them to "talk to the hand" because you know that teachers are great. Say to them, "Stop in the name of learning! I have no listening for you. You're breaking up. Children can learn, and teachers can teach. Now step off from me!"

Keep a gratitude journal for every day. At the end of the day write down at least three things you can think of that worked for you that day. Decide on your minimum number and stay true to that. Here is the secret: Be grateful for events, gifts that happened THAT DAY ONLY. This strategy keeps you from getting stuck in automatic responses like "I'm grateful for my job, my life, my car . . ." Your gratitudes will be juicier and more expansive like, "I am grateful for the rainbow on the wall from the geometric prism, the fresh green shoot on our classroom plant, the croaking of our pet frog to tell us the fresh rains are near." Take note of miracles, like when a concept "clicks" for a student.

**NOW THAT YOU ARE READY TO TAKE ACTION ON SOME OF THE STRATEGIES MENTIONED IN THE STORIES, HERE ARE SOME CONCRETE SUGGESTIONS THAT YOU CAN USE IN YOUR CLASSROOM. ENJOY!**

## Chapter One: "A Lovely Day"

❧ Make your classroom learning environment as aesthetically pleasing as possible. Place beautiful plants, artifacts, and reproductions of artwork by famous artists like Jacob Lawrence and Van Gogh in your space. Trust the children with beautiful things. Teach them how to handle and take care of them.

❧ Set up a silver tea service or any kind of tea pot and cups that you would like. Teach the children a consistent, step-by-step procedure for serving tea and washing the china. Get china from a thrift store.

❧ Bring in fresh flowers that a florist has disposed of as "distressed" goods and let the children arrange them. The florist will give you a great price on them or give them to you free.

## Chapter Two: "Peter and the Po'k Chops"

❧ Share a "We're in it to win it" attitude with your students. Let them know that you are on their side and that you will not let them fail. Choose students for competitions and give everyone a chance to support the students. Everyone wins.

❧ Cook something in the classroom for your students or bring something you made from home. (Be aware of your fire codes, the school's food policies, and children's allergies.) You can also order food in from a restaurant.

❧ Maintain high standards of respectful dress. Applaud students who take pride in looking groomed. It's not about the designer labels. It's about clean, crisp, and professional. They are professional students.

## Chapter Three: "Who Put the Worm in Green Slime on My Desk?"

🎋 Immerse students in quality, classical literature.

🎋 Play the "Rummage Sale Game." Have students bring in something that might be junk to one person but treasure to another. Have students write a composition about it and share out loud.

🎋 Share stories about when you made a wrong assumption about something.

## Chapter Four: "From Community Helpers to the Big Island"

🎋 Take different routes into school and notice what buildings, businesses, and places of interest are there.

🎋 Attend an event in your school community after work. Introduce yourself to the people attending.

🎋 Study the history of your school community. Get out and explore.

## Chapter Five: "We're Off to See the Bad People"

🎋 Travel to nontraditional places on field trips.

🎋 Go teach in an environment totally different from what you already know.

🎋 Listen to what students are saying and let their interests or misinformation guide your instruction.

## Chapter Six: "Mice in the Classroom, Men in Space"

🦶 Put out a variety of materials and let the children create something.

🦶 Allow for "down time" and make way for the children to lead. Record what happens and develop a wonderful learning theme or unit.

🦶 Play along with the students' creative spirits. You don't always have to be the authority figure. Laugh at yourself.

## Chapter Seven: "Creating the Glittery Glass Bottle Tree"

🦶 Take a Broadway musical or an art exhibit that you enjoyed and develop it into a teaching unit.

🦶 Reflect on what your "glitter" is, the thing that brings you joy, and use it or do it.

🦶 Research an old tradition from your culture and build a unit of study around it.

## Chapter Eight: "I'll Never Teach Another Day . . . Until Tomorrow"

🦶 Bring an animal into the classroom so that the children can study zoology and learn about responsibility, as well.

🦶 Write some favorite quotations that inspire you and place them where you can read them so they can "light you up" every day.

🦶 Nurture yourself with massages, bubble baths, playing golf, shooting hoops, watching the game on TV, or whatever you do to relax. Put a little environmental waterfall in your classroom. If you feel you need it, schedule yourself a meltdown tantrum and then suit up and show up at school the next day renewed and ready to get the job done.

## Chapter Nine: "Catch That Monk, He's Falling"

🔥 Play a game called "What boys can do, what girls can do." Ask your students about careers or roles to uncover inaccurate beliefs your students might have about what the sexes can and cannot accomplish.

🔥 Teach children to apologize authentically and also teach the offended child to say "I forgive you." Those are very powerful and healing words. Do not force the child to apologize until he is ready.

🔥 Create a "Fortunately Journal" and an "Unfortunately Journal" in two composition notebooks (I like the black and white speckled ones with the sewn binding, not spiral wire). When you don't have time to listen to good news or tattling, encourage the child to go write the incident he is trying to tell you in the Fortunately Journal or the Unfortunately Journal. Assure the child that he can read what he wrote to you later. (Be sure to make time to read what the child has written and to respond.)

## Chapter Ten: "Go With the Flow, Even If It's Pee"

🔥 Acknowledge students who speak and listen well in public. Plan a symposium and let the students have a discussion on a topic of interest. Have your own performances in the classroom at the end of the day and invite parents and friends.

🔥 Choose a book that you love and plan a fun, extended writing activity around it. Get others in the community involved in your fun.

🔥 Take the students to visit a senior citizens' independent living facility and let the students read to the residents or present a play or performance.

## Chapter Eleven: "$100,000 Teacher"

When you hear of an award for a teacher, nominate a colleague or nominate yourself. If there is a grant available to further your work, go for it. The answer to your request might be "yes" or "no" or "maybe so." If you don't write a grant, you already have your answer.

E-mail me at whyweteach@gmail.com and tell me about your successes and how you have used some of my ideas.

> *"And if you get the choice to sit it out or dance, DANCE!*
> *I hope you . . . dance!" (Lee Ann Womack)*

It has been my honor to share my teaching thoughts, stories, and philosophies with you. Don't take any of my suggestions as though they were written in stone. Enhance them, enrich them, and make them your own. Hang tough, but be flexible. Enjoy your teaching journey. This is not a dress rehearsal—this is it. How good are you willing to have it be? Thank you for loving generously and "playing big" for our children. Asé.

# Why I Teach

*Reprise: "The seeds of transformation I plant will yield a bountiful harvest."*

જ઼ા

**BEN CEFKIN**
Denver School of the Arts
Major: Instrumental
Music/Ethnomusicology
*Year in my class: 1994*

**PARIS KEELING**
Denver East High School
Focus: College-prep,
cheerleading
*Years in my class: 1995 and 2001*

**PHAEDRA LUCKETT**
Langston University
Major: English education
*Years in my class: 1990–1993*

**STERLING MURPHY**
Denver East High School
Focus: Music; vocalist
*Years in my class: 1995 and 2001*

**WILL SIMMONS**
Texas Southern University
Major: Economics
*Year in my class: 1990*

**ERICA K. WORMLEY**
University of Wyoming
Major: Elementary education
*Year in my class: 1991*

RUBY WHITE
University of Northern Colorado
Major: Psychology
*Years in my class: 1991–1994*

KIMBERLY KAEUPER
Kindergarten teacher
*Years in my class: 1988 and 1989*

ALLISON CONNER
Rice University pre-med program
Majors: Biochemistry and Hispanic studies
*Year in my class: 1992*

NICOLO ONORATO
Television production specialist
*Year in my class: 1985*

RAFAEL EUGENE DERR
University of Colorado at Denver
Major: Political science and Chicano studies
*Years in my class: 1992–1995*

JULIE DESAI
Cardiothoracic surgery physician assistant
*Years in my class: 1984–1987*

# Afterword

We can teach our children to count from one to ten,

to name the colors of the rainbow

and the days of the week.

We can teach them to name letters,

to write their names

and to recognize onsets and rimes.

We can teach them to line up,

to raise their hands before speaking,

to sit in a chair and stay on task.

We can teach them to recognize the phases of the moon

and continents on the globe

and the states within the boundaries of our nation,

and it will all be for nothing

if we fail to keep their basic human dignity intact.

We fail them when we take their dignity

and strip away the layers of self worth

that enable them to value other human beings,

all of whom are more like one another than different from one
    another.

We fail them when we behave as if others can, but they cannot.

We fail them when we treat them as if others are more worthy

and they are less so, for whatever reasons.

We fail them when we allow ourselves to become entangled

in the web of stereotypes and alter our expectations
even before we meet them.

I am filled with a hope that brings me great joy
as I read the last pages of this collection of stories
and strategies and bits of wisdom.
I want to place this book in the hands of every teacher,
especially those in their first years of our profession.
Linda Alston is a mentor for us,
a living demonstration of the influence of treating others
as you would have them treat you.
She has shown what can happen when children are trusted,
guided with dignity,
treated as fully worthy simply because they inhale and exhale.

Linda leads us to notice what can happen
when we remove the blinders of stereotypes
and the harness of sliding expectations
to give young children a more robust view of the world.

She opens our eyes to the richness of life in her classroom
as she opens the eyes of children
to a world bigger than the limitations of their own existence.
Linda reminds us that this is equally important
for children of great wealth and privilege
as it is for the children of poverty and need.
She and her children show how respect and caring,
truth and trust, open minds and open hearts

are as essential to learning

as planning and lessons and curriculum and assessment.


Linda reminds us of what is truly important in our profession.

At a time when others are being sucked into the quicksand of
distraction,

she continues to live with her children

in a classroom focused on rituals and routines

that give them structure in a chaotic world,

structure that offers a sense of safety in knowing what comes next.

She leads them to understand that loving one another,

honoring themselves and their families,

and respecting their communities can help them be grounded when
they face a challenge.

Linda understands the importance of grace and elegance,

respect and civility to the healthy development of her children.

Perhaps most important,

Linda understands that she is growing not only the minds of her
students,

but that she is also growing the hearts and souls

of her fellow human beings.

—Lester L. Laminack, author and literacy consultant,
Asheville, NC